THE DEVELOPING SCHOOL

School Development and the Management of Change Series

Series Editors: Peter Holly and Geoff Southworth
Cambridge Institute of Education
Cambridge, CB2 2BX, UK

School Development and the Management of Change Series: 1

THE DEVELOPING SCHOOL

Peter Holly and
Geoff Southworth

The Falmer Press
(A member of the Taylor & Francis Group)
London • New York • Philadelphia

UK The Falmer Press, Falmer House, Barcombe, Lewes, East Sussex, BN8 5DL

USA The Falmer Press, Taylor & Francis Inc., 242 Cherry Street, Philadelphia, PA 19106-1906

First published 1989

British Library Cataloguing in Publication Data

Holly, Peter
The Developing school.—(School development and the management of change series: 1)
1. Schools. Management
I. Title. II. Southworth, Geoff. III. Series
371.2
ISBN 1-85000-484-6
ISBN 1-85000-485-4 (pbk.)

Jacket design by Caroline Archer

Typeset in 12/13 Garamond by
The FD Group Ltd, Fleet, Hampshire

Printed in Great Britain by Taylor & Francis (Printers) Ltd, Basingstoke

Contents

Acknowledgments

We would like to express our gratitude to all those teachers with whom we have worked on the ideas contained in this book. Without their practical efforts, this book would not have been possible. Thank you, then, to teachers in Bromley, Cambridgeshire, Enfield, Grampian, Hertfordshire, the Inner London Education Authority, Northamptonshire and Suffolk.

This book is dedicated to all those teachers
who are developing their schools

Introduction

In producing this book our intention was to provide some practical guidelines for teachers to use as they attempted to develop their schools. What we have tried to put together is a practical framework for school development. At the same time we have also sought to underpin the framework with insights, observations and findings from school-based researchers and developers. We have drawn upon our own experiences of school development, and those of colleagues in Britain and North America. Importantly, we have made use of the responses and feelings of teachers with whom we have worked on courses and in schools. Everything outlined in the following pages is already happening in schools around us. What we have tried to do is synthesize this practical experience.

In synthesizing all this material we have been struck by one thing — how wide-ranging the task of school development is. In one very real sense school development is sprawling since it involves the melding and blending of several key tasks notably: leadership; curriculum coordination; evaluation; staff development; and teaching and learning. Consequently, a chapter is devoted to each of these areas with the exception of teaching and learning. This does not have a chapter of its own because it is mentioned in all of the chapters: it is the thread which binds the book together. After all, if school development does not affect teaching and learning is the school really developing?

To say that school development is wide-ranging is also to acknowledge that the process involves risk, ambiguity, uncertainty and hard work. Whilst we have attempted to pull together a large number of ideas and suggestions, we have resisted and, hopefully, avoided reducing the enterprise into too tidy a process. We have kept in mind the comments of Ann Lieberman (1985) when she said:

> After all the National Reports on Education have been read, analyzed, praised, and critiqued, there will be the crying need to figure out how to improve schools to make them better places for both the adults who come to teach and the young ones who come to learn. Schools are complex organizations; we therefore need complex ways of thinking about them.

We acknowledge this complexity by discussing the key tasks in some detail and by reflecting some of the dilemmas and problems raised in developing and managing change. In the face of complexity we have not opted for simplicity. In some cases we may have simplified some of the issues but we have consistently sought to avoid being simplistic. One of the things which teachers have told us, and which our own experiences of living and working in schools supports, is that school development, especially in the early stages, is complicated, subtle and, perhaps above all else, messy rather than neat and tidy.

As a way through this messiness, and to help staff find a way around the thickets, brambles and pitfalls of doing school development, we advocate careful and sensitive planning. Moreover, such planning should be about the school planning its own development. School development plans are, we believe, the best way forward. Thus chapter 2, which presents our (and others) thinking about school development plans, is a central chapter to the book, so saying we also recognize that school development plans will be central to the implementation and institutionalization of the national curriculum.

On the surface the philosophy which informs this book may appear to sit uncomfortably with externally imposed change. To some extent this is true. At various points we say that school development does stem and should stem from within each school. Yet, it is also true that no school is an island. During the 1980s much has been going on which has been primarily concerned with altering the school's autonomy and relationship with its environment (for example, legislation in respect of the role of school governors, LEAs, central government). Any developing school puts itself in peril if it ignores the context and community in which it operates. Developing schools need to be simultaneously 'inside' and 'outside' focussed. Furthermore, whatever one might believe about the politics of the post-1988 context, school development and the implementation of a National Curriculum and its subsequent review are not in conflict. It is our contention that the implementation of the National Curriculum rests substantially upon the principles, ideas and approaches we outline in this book. Although the book was never conceived as a tool of the National Curriculum Council we believe our approach to school development, with its emphasis upon the development process, is of some utility to schools engaged upon the interpretation and implementation of National Curriculum Council reports. It is all a matter of emphasis and we are foremost interested in schools and what they might need to do. We see this book as serving *schools* as they strive to come to terms with the new age.

This present volume is intended to stand in its own right. However, it also serves a second purpose. It is the lead book in a new series entitled 'School Development and the Management of Change'. Many of the themes featured in this book will be interwoven throughout the series and, indeed, amplified in the various contributions. The series will emphasize the development of primary schools but will contain much of relevance for secondary schools and will feature aspects of school development in the UK, but not exclusively so. Indeed, two volumes in the series — those prepared by Ann Lieberman and Michael Fullan — arise from current work in North America. Nevertheless, contributors to the series share some central priorities. The prime focus across the series is school improvement, or, as we prefer to call it, school development. Another concern is how to make it happen, i.e. the mechanics of the reform process, particularly the ins and outs of the management of change. Management *for* change (see Goodchild and Holly, 1989) is the stuff of this series. Moreover, change management is not the sole preserve of senior staff in schools. Leadership, as Southworth (1988) has pointed out, is not necessarily the property of the privileged few; it is the right and the responsibility of us all. We would contend, therefore, that this book in particular, and the ensuing series in general, is of relevance to all teachers. For school development to occur, all teachers must become school developers. Accordingly, we hope that this book and all the subsequent books in the series will provide valuable assistance along the way and thus fulfil the practical purposes for which they are intended.

Peter Holly
Geoff Southworth
Cambridge, March 1989

Chapter 1

The Learning School

Welcome to 'The Developing School' — your school. We would like to be able to invite you to climb aboard but, of course, you already are on board. Your school has developed, is developing and will develop. Whether you have any control over this process, however, is another matter. A key theme of this book is teacher empowerment, one aspect of which is having a sense of purchase on the change process. School development, therefore, is self-development. It is the development of your school by you and your colleagues. Much as we would like to invite you to sit back and watch the moving story, this is not what school development is about. You have to move the story; you have to make it happen. It is far more commonplace than any *Magical Mystery Tour.* All too often, perhaps, we have been tempted to look at school development as somewhat magical and rather mysterious. What we are offering here is an alternative scenario; one in which school development is demystified. Rather than being something which comes to you and is done to you by outsiders, the 'experts', we see it as something which is done by you and for you, the insiders, with appropriate outside help and in the light of external-imposed obligations. In this alternative scenario we are all experts — in different ways. We all have something important to offer. Having said this, we would also argue that school development — if it is to be successful and productive — has to become your way of life and pursued according to a particular style, your style, your 'house style'. This book is all about this style — and how to generate it. It is vital that it becomes your style — that your school acquires what we refer to below as a **development culture,** which, in relation to other schools, embodies both similarity and difference and an internal capacity for moving forward.

The Developing School Revolves Around, and is Energized by, its Development Culture

Central to the themes of this book is our argument that the development culture is created by the acquisition of three interrelated aspects; the full potency of which is only realized when they are working together — in combination.

A school can be said to have a development culture when it possesses:

(i) an organic and cyclical approach which rests on various development processes;
(ii) a repertoire of techniques and strategies which can be skilfully and artfully utilized to mobilize the processes referred to above;
(iii) the ability on the part of the staff to work together in collaboration in order to promote development.

The development culture, therefore, is both process and technique and rests on a culture of collaboration. In this book we want to explore these three aspects of school development.

To give an early example — and one which will be followed up later in this book — **evaluation** (or, more appropriately, self-evaluation) is a corner-stone of school development.

The Developing School is the Evaluative School

As we will outline in a later chapter, the cyclical nature of school development revolves around what are essentially evaluation processes within which a repertoire of evaluation techniques can be utilized. And, at best, evaluation is a collaborative activity. It provides the substance of collaborative inquiry.

Evaluation, then, is a spanning activity; it entails the application of both processes and techniques within a team orientation. In so doing, it integrates the three aspects of the development culture.

Learning is another example of a spanning activity.

The Developing School is the Learning School

The Learning School

Essentially, the Learning School is a place that works for both children and adults; it is a place 'designed for learning'. We have borrowed this phrase from 'Ten Good Schools: A Secondary School Enquiry by HMI'. We would argue, however, that it is a pertinent phrase for all developing schools, whether they are primary, middle or secondary. The same report emphasizes that what 'good' schools have in common is effective leadership and a climate that is conducive to growth. Such schools, HMI argue:

> see themselves as places **designed for learning;** they take trouble to make their philosophies explicit for themselves and to explain them to parents and pupils; the foundation of their work and corporate life is an acceptance of shared values.
>
> Emphasis is laid on consultation, team work and participation, but, without exception, the most single factor in the success of these schools is the quality of leadership of the head. Without exception, the heads have qualities of imagination and vision, tempered by realism, which have enabled them to sum up not only their present situation but also attainable future goals. They appreciate the need for specific educational aims, both social and intellectual, and have the capacity to communicate these to staff, pupils and parents, to win their assent and to put their own policies into practice. Their sympathetic understanding of staff and pupils, their accessibility, good humour and sense of proportion and their dedication to their task has won them the respect of parents, teachers and taught. They are conscious of the corruption of power and though ready to take final responsibility they have made power-sharing the keynote of their organization and administration. Such leadership is crucial for success and these schools are what their heads and staffs have made them (DES, 1977).

Contained in this quotation are several themes touched upon in this chapter and, indeed, in the remainder of this volume. What is clear, however, is that 'leadership for learning' is indispensable. Indeed, we would argue that the Learning School has five interrelated characteristics. In the Learning School:

- the focus is on children and their learning;

- individual teachers are encouraged to be continuing learners themselves;
- the group of teachers (and sometimes others) who constitute the 'staff' is encouraged to collaborate by learning with and from each other;
- the school (i.e. all those people who constitute the 'school') learns its way forward. The school as an organization is a 'learning system' (see Schon, 1971).
- the headteacher is the leading learner.

In other words, in the Learning School, learning is

- what children do;
- what teachers do;
- what the staff does;
- what the school as an organization does;
- what the headteacher does.

It is worth stressing that *learning* is about *doing;* it is what everybody *does* in the Learning School, albeit at various levels in the organization. Indeed, these levels are encompassed within this quotation from The Carnegie Report (1986):

> The focus of schooling must shift from teaching to learning, from the passive acquisition of facts and routines to the active application of ideas to problems. This transition makes the role of the teacher more important, not less. Teachers must think for themselves if they are to help others think for themselves, be able to act independently and *collaborate with others,* and render critical judgment. (What is required is) a transformation of the environment for teaching. School systems based on bureaucratic authority must be replaced by schools in which authority is grounded in the professional competence of the teacher, and where teachers work together as colleagues, constantly striving to improve their performance . . .

What follows is an elaboration of these 'levels of learning'.

Level 1: Children's learning

The aim is to teach for children and their learning; to facilitate and maximize the learning of each and every child in the school. It is vital to have a purchase on both the nature of the learning process and the extent and quality of learning outcomes. The understanding here is that, when we know more about the ins and outs of learning, then we can begin to teach accordingly. As has been said previously,

> The teacher needs to learn from the learner how to teach and to teach the learner how to learn.

It could be argued, therefore, that this represents a subtle shift of emphasis; whereas the previous focus was on *teaching*, the focus now is on *learning*. At a basic level learning involves:

> acquiring some knowledge or a skill — knowing what and knowing how;
> committing something to memory;
> becoming aware from observation;
> becoming informed;
> understanding more about something.

While these are some of the aspects of learning, many commentators are paying more and more attention to styles of learning, including the elevation of both experiential learning and enquiry learning alongside more basic approaches. As a consequence there has been much emphasis placed on the importance of engaging the pupils in more active learning, problem-solving and practical investigations. Indeed, when it comes to learning, variety may well be the spice of life. Holly (1986) has drawn a map of the key linkages in learning (see below), while the much used paragraph 243 from the Cockcroft Report has recommended a combination of learning styles:

> Mathematics teaching at all levels should include opportunities for
>
> > exposition by the teacher;
> > discussion between teacher and pupils and between pupils themselves;
> > appropriate practical work;
> > consolidation and practice of fundamental skills and routines;
> > problem-solving, including the application of mathematics to everyday situations;
> > investigational work.
>
> In setting out this list we are aware that we are not saying anything which has not already been said many times and over many years. The list which we have given has appeared, by implication if not explicitly, in official reports, DES publica-

> tions, HMI discussion papers and journals and publications of the professional mathematical associations. Yet we are aware that although there are some classrooms in which the teaching includes, as a matter of course, all the elements which we have listed, there are still many in which the mathematics teaching does not include even a majority of these elements.

Our contention is that this quotation has a relevance across the whole curriculum.

Figure 1: Key linkages in learning

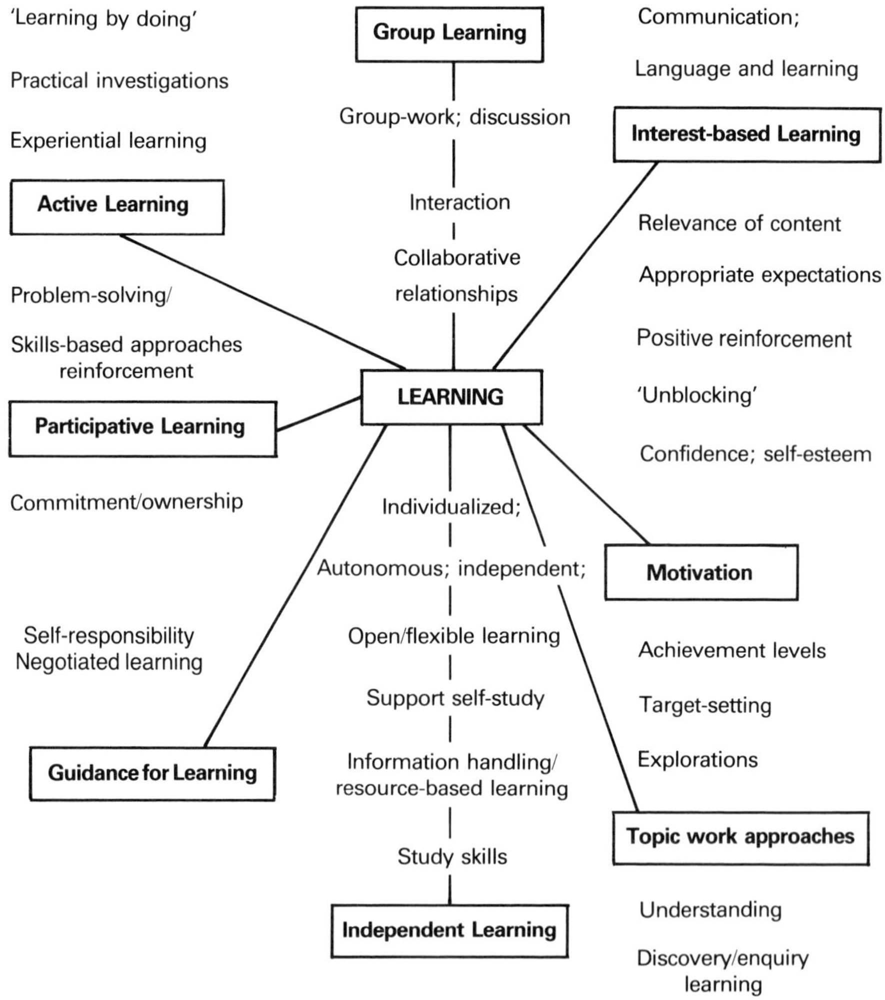

In 1985 our colleague, Ted Brennan, surveyed the developments taking place in the 14-19 curriculum and concluded that there was much that was happening which had a 'primary flavour':

> In a curious way, one hears echoes of the professional debates in the late '60s concerning Plowden philosophy in the primary schools. There is an uncanny resemblance between the spirit of child-centred primary education . . . and the student-centred philosophy that seems to underpin so much of pre-vocational thinking at the present time. The development of skills, learning through experience, group activity with its opportunities for discussion, the importance of good record-keeping as a corollary — it is all there.

We want to ask, however, whether his description of classroom practice in the primary school (involving experiential learning, group work, skill acquisition and record-keeping) is rhetoric or reality. Generally speaking, does it constitute the effective (i.e. received/actual) curriculum; or is there a performance gap between the rhetorical curriculum and the curriculum as experienced by the children?

In 1970 John Goodlad and Francis Klein published their findings arising from extensive research in American elementary school classrooms. Their main discovery was that the rhetoric of innovation of the 1960s was not being matched by changes in classroom practice. Indeed, schools were curiously unaffected by the plethora of innovations being promoted at that point in time.

In terms of their research, Goodlad and Klein used twelve indicators to record the shape of classroom life. These indicators provide a useful set of dimensions for classroom observation:

- **milieu:** the learning environment and the climate of the classroom;
- **instructional activities:** the kinds of teaching and learning styles being used;
- **subject matter:** the focus and content of pupil learning;
- **materials/equipment:** resources for learning;
- **involvement:** the level of the children's (and teacher's) interest, enthusiasm and engagement;
- **interaction:** whether the pupils are active or passive learners;
- **enquiry:** whether the learning process is open or closed;
- **independence:** the degree of freedom or control being exercised in the learning situation;
- **curriculum balance:** the range of experiences being covered;

- **curricular adaptation:** whether curriculum 'packages' are being used and to what extent they have been modified to suit the particular circumstances of the classroom;
- **expectations:** the appropriateness of the individual levels of attainment established by the teacher;
- **staff relationships:** whether the teachers exist in isolation from each other or are able to enter into a collegial, team approach to their classroom responsibilities.

In using these indicators, Goodlad and Klein found much evidence of 'innovation without change'. They came across a veneer of innovation under which there continued to exist long-established classroom practices. This mismatch between the rhetoric and reality of learning is a central concern in the Learning School. The concern is with the gap between the classroom aspirations of the teachers and the fruits of their labours. But Goodlad and Klein found themselves investigating the nature of a different gap; that between external expectations and internal performances. In the Learning School the teachers are encouraged to set their own goals (and, in so doing, to countenance external demands) and then to review the nature and extent of their achievements. In the Learning School the teachers — the professionals in the situation — have the prime responsibility for the learning of the children in their classrooms.

And the Learning School becomes the Developing School when the teachers accept that their 'underlying purpose is to improve the teaching and learning process in the school' (quoted in the GRIDS handbooks).

Level 2: Teacher learning

Teachers themselves are continuing learners; they can continue to learn about their craft, about the classroom and about the needs of the children. Teachers can learn by looking at learning.

In North America there is currently much talk about the establishment of **professional development schools.** If they are nothing else, these are schools which encourage staff members to develop professionally on a continuing basis. The foundation of such schools reflects a deliberate attempt to place the emphasis where it needs to be placed — on the core activity, i.e. teaching for learning. As has been remarked recently, within the burgeoning literature on effective schools (on both sides of the Atlantic), there is a curious silence concerning the process of teaching and learning. The interest in effective schools, emanates from what Gary Sykes (1988) has called a 'management ideology' which fails to promote the importance of establishing more adventuresome, inspired, engaged and effective (as opposed to merely efficient) classroom teaching. Professional development schools are designed to promote the centrality of classroom processes, while acknowledging that the improvement of children's learning rests on the success of teacher learning.

We would equate teacher learning with their continuing professional education. It is the essence of professional development, aside from their personal (career) needs, teachers as professionals need to keep abreast of new developments, extend their expertise and acquire new competencies. Joyce and Showers (1980) have usefully differentiated between teachers having to 'fine tune' skills that they already possess and then having to add entirely new skills to their repertoires of teaching strategies. Taken together, these constitute the substance of professional growth. As Rubin (1978) has remarked:

> Any attempt to improve children's learning depends on some form of teacher growth . . . However good a practitioner's preservice preparation may be, continual readjustments in educational goals and procedures impose new demands on craftsmanship. (Accordingly) skills are mastered, and new knowledge is utilized, through continuous personal striving toward greater proficiency.

In addition, Rubin emphasizes the importance of professional **development:** it is a question, he says, of cultivating professional artistry:

> Teaching is a performing art; therefore it is developed — like all other performing arts — through prolonged and intelligent practice . . . Gifted teachers rarely come ready-made. They possess a finely-honed intuition, a capacity to develop understanding out of ordinary experience, and an ability to provoke genuine thinking in their students. They are problem-solvers rather than rule-followers; creative rather than ritualistic; visionary rather than myopic; real rather than pretentious; and demanding rather than easily-satisfied. Above all, they are driven not only by ideals but by a corresponding passion for engineering their realization.

While such teachers provide the 'crew' for the Learning School (and, indeed, the Developing School), according to Joyce and Showers, they only become 'wonderful learners' when they are placed in conducive settings for staff development. In other words, such teachers require a sympathetic environment when they themselves are in a learning situation. As Rubin (1978) underlines, such growing professionals would not take kindly to 'corrective' training. They demand a more enlightened approach to professional development. Consequently, he says,

> the best teachers must have periodic occasions for reflection, for readjusting their tactics to shifting social situations, and for utilizing new processes and procedures.

These same teachers are often referred to as **reflective practitioners.** They are prepared to confront the 'performance gap' between their intentions and their accomplishments in the classroom. They agree with Stenhouse (1975) that,

> the gap can be closed only by adopting a research and development approach to one's own teaching, whether alone or in a group of cooperating teachers.

And these 'cooperating teachers' work together on the process of **collaborative enquiry**.

Level 3: Collaborative learning

Teachers are increasingly learning together — in collaboration. And they use evaluation techniques to learn their way forward. As developers and implementers, they are learning all the time. And they are increasingly learning how to learn from each other (see Fullan, 1985). This new enthusiasm explains the current popularity of visiting (one's own school or someone else's), work shadowing, paired observation, teaming, coaching, and 'professional chaining' (see Holly and Newman, 1988). All these activities are based on learning as a reciprocal and mutual process.

Toynbee (1987) maintains, however, that teacher autonomy — and isolation — is declining, albeit slowly. As late as 1982, she says, the DES was able to report that,

> . . . in 45 (out of the 80 first schools surveyed in England) there was either no explicit policy or it was believed that each teacher should determine his or her own classroom organization and approaches to learning.

Like Richards (1987) and Holly and Martin (1987), however, Toynbee sees the gradual demise of teacher autonomy as a positive trend, especially as the corollary is the upsurge in teacher collaboration and more coherent curriculum planning. As evidence of this more corporate approach, she cites the deployment of curriculum coordinators in primary schools. Such 'consultants' are charged with the responsibility of converting their own, and outside knowledge, into something used by the whole staff. Curriculum guidelines, for instance, become the common property of the staff at large. It is a case, then, of leading the staff into collaboration. Moreover, Toynbee is able to list some of the benefits of a more cooperative approach; she mentions

- more economical use of resources;
- the fusion of individual enthusiasms and expertise into team-based endeavours;
- the creation of opportunities for subject integration and, therefore, cross-curricular initiatives;
- the establishment of frameworks for progression, continuity and liaison;
- the active involvement of classroom teachers in the making of a more meaningful, coherent and constantly evolving curriculum;
- the recognition of the importance of in-house teacher support;
- the generation of staff participation in school-based development;
- the emergence of a more confident and trusting collegial team.

Collaborative learning, then, is now seen as a cornerstone of the Learning School. Indeed, in the form of collaborative enquiry, it provides the **linkage** for integrating the five levels of learning. Collaborative enquiry is the crux of the matter. And one of its central features is **teaming.**

'Teaming', as a concept, is normally used to mean team-teaching. We would want to use a broader definition of the term. To us, teaming is the heart-beat of the collaborative school. It is constituted by the readiness of staff members to join together to form investigative 'interest groups' or participative problem-solving teams. As Goodlad and Klein (1970) have emphasized, whatever the size of the school, teaming is part and parcel of a whole school response to curriculum renewal:

> If a school-wide programme of curriculum reconstruction is undertaken, it is necessary that there be widespread faculty participation . . .
>
> In a small faculty, the staff may work as a committee of the whole . . . the entire staff, when small, may also operate as a committee of the whole to formulate its philosophy of education and to work out a statement of psychology of learning. Then the

> staff, as a whole, can use these results in selecting the objectives for the school . . .
>
> Larger schools will find it necessary to operate as special committees . . .
>
> Although a school-wide attack is preferable in getting a rational revision of the curriculum, improvements can be made if only a part of the instructional programme can be dealt with. Thus, curriculum-building can be undertaken for a single subject like mathematics, or a single grade . . . or even for the courses offered by an individual teacher.

But teaming, like staff collaboration itself, is only one element in the learning package. Indeed, we would argue that collaborative learning is necessary but not sufficient for organizational learning.

Level 4: Organizational learning

The Learning School as an organization learns its way forward. Such an organization has the capacity to learn:

> how to develop from the inside;
> how to develop internally by responding to demands from the outside;
> how to anticipate the shape of the future.

There are various aspects of this kind of organizational learning:

(a) like the 'Listening Bank', the Learning School needs to listen to the messages emanating from both its immediate community and its wider environment. It needs to be both reactive and proactive and eager to find an 'ecological niche' for itself (see Goodchild and Holly, 1989). According to Bennis and Nanus (1985), schools as organizations have to learn how to operate in new modes and, as a consequence, they have to be constantly transforming themselves and increasing their readiness to cope with new opportunities. Above all, however, the Learning School has to be **adaptive.** What is required, say Patterson *et al* (1986), is

> an organization that can adapt and adopt, if the organization is to be innovative, productive, and of high quality.

(b) as Bennis and Nanus (1985) contend,

> some organizational learning occurs whenever a group of people is engaged in a common enterprise.

Nevertheless, a major task is to be able to integrate individual and small group enterprise on behalf of the enterprise — the school. Both integration and staff deployment are crucial here. Consequently, Patterson *et al* (1986) claim that,

> a good organization is flexible, uses integrated structures, monitors itself (and its) organizational culture, develops strategic planning techniques and empowers its people.

While there are learning parts in a learning system, it can be argued that organizational learning occurs on a different plain. Consider these quotations from Bennis and Nanus (1985) and Argyris and Schon (1978) respectively.

> Organizational learning is the process by which an organization obtains and uses new knowledge, tools, behaviours, and values. It happens at all levels in the organization — among individuals and groups as well as system-wide. Individuals learn as part of their daily activities, particularly as they interact with each other and the outside world. Groups learn as their members cooperate to accomplish common goals. The entire system learns as it obtains feedback from the environment and anticipates further changes. At all levels, newly learned knowledge is translated into new goals, procedures, expectations, role structures, and measures of success.

> . . . It is clear that organizational learning is not the same thing as individual learning, even when the individuals who learn are members of the organization. There are too many cases in which organizations know less than their members. There are even cases in which the organization cannot seem to learn what everybody knows. Nor does it help to think of organizational learning as the prerogative of a man at the top who learns for the organization.

Besides deployment/empowerment and integration, other concepts such as knowledge utilization and dissemination and orchestration are clearly important. Information needs to be communicated across the organization. Moreover, a balanced approach is also required. Holly (in Reid, Hopkins and Holly, 1987) has described the need to develop at the individual, team and organizational levels. While the development work does not have to operate on all levels simultaneously, there is a need for both communication across the levels and orchestration of activities so that one level is not over-emphasized at the expense of the others. Traditionally, the organizational level has been neglected (thus resulting in over-developed individuals in under-developed schools); presently, there is some evidence that the pendulum may have swung too far to the organizational dimension at the expense of the individual. Evidently, there is a need for a **balance of interests** within an organization.

Figure 2: The cycle of school-based improvement through self-evaluation

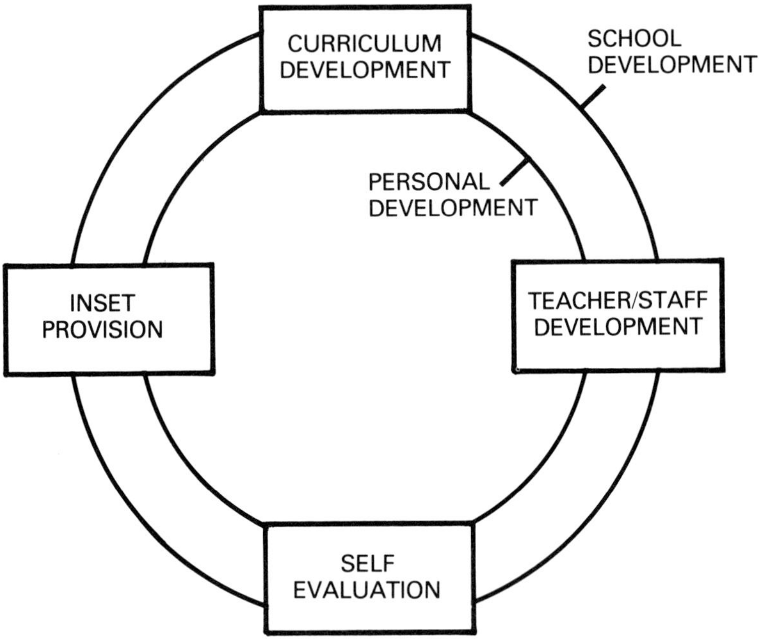

(c) The Learning School, if it is to be an adaptive, self-balancing and self-managing organization, needs enough autonomy for it to be sufficiently self-determining — and, indeed, if it is to be afforded the status of an 'independent learner'. Timar and Kirp (1987), in describing the kind of **institutional competence** that is required for effective educational reform, have concluded that,

> reform is most needed where learning takes place — in the individual schools, in the classroom, and in the interaction between teacher and student. As businesses world-wide have learned, problems can best be solved at the lowest level of operation. While structures are needed, bureaucracies tend to focus on rules and regulations rather than results, thus stifling

> initiative. Therefore, we believe that school governance should be retained at the local level . . .

Not only, then, does the organization need to have certain conditions within which its learning orientation can be fostered but also these same conditions must be established for all those learners — children and adults alike — inside the organization. This is, therefore, a symmetrical relationship between the conditions for learning inside and outside a school as an organization. And, as Patterson *et al* (1986) have pointed out, the orientation is also a **process** one:

> . . . the ultimate reason for mobilizing energy in the first place is to affect children's learning. The decentralization of decision-making power places the clout to make things happen as close to the action as possible . . . Success in non-rational systems is measured by the ability to mobilize energy to get things done in an effective way. The watchword is not so much product as process.

While children are experiencing the process of learning, their teachers are learning about the process of innovation and how to implement classroom changes effectively — in order to enhance the learning of the children. And as Berman and McLaughlin (1976), Fullan (1985) and Weick (1976) have argued, successful implementation (and teacher learning within this process) demands a certain kind of organization — the school as a 'loosely coupled system'. Hargreaves (1982 and 1988) has made much the same points. He has argued that children should be given responsibility for their own learning, encouraged to take risks and to learn from their mistakes, and enabled to be participative, active and self-assessing learners. Positive reinforcement, he says, should underpin life in the classroom. Moreover, he argues, schools as organizations should be run like classrooms. Authority dependency is to be avoided; diversity and enterprise celebrated. And central to classrooms and schools is the quality of the prevailing **climate.**

(d) Many commentators including Holly (1989), Torrington *et al* (1987) and Deal and Kennedy (1983) have argued that the quality of an institution is in large part dependent on the quality of its organizational climate (or culture). Halpin's pioneering work in the 1960s centred on such indicators as esprit, engagement, hindrance, intimacy, aloofness, consideration, thrust, and productivity. Campbell *et al* weighed in with the following dimensions:

> task structure (the degree to which the methods used to

accomplish tasks are spelled out;
reward-punishment relationship;
decision centralization;
achievement emphasis;
training versus development emphasis;
security versus risk;
openness versus defensiveness;
status and morale;
recognition and feedback;
general organizational competence and flexibility.

While this is a more comprehensive list than that offered by Halpin and Croft (1982), it covers much the same ground. What is clear from both sets of indicators/dimensions is that an organization's 'climate' or culture is of central importance. Campbell *et al* (1971), for instance, stress not only the level of organizational competence and flexibility but also the school's capacity to pursue its goals in a flexible, innovative, anticipatory, adaptive and **developmental** mode. Hoyle (1975) described the 'creative school' as one capable of self-renewal, of acting as an agency of change, and of planning for change. He added that the quality of a school as an institution is crucial to the success of an innovation. And in the DES/HMI document entitled 'Ten Good Schools' a school's climate was singled out for particular attention. The factors which were said to be vital included conduciveness for growth, shared values, consultation, team-work, participation, power-sharing, delegation and vision. Clearly an organizational climate is closely related to the style of management exercised in a school and its level of corporate functioning. What is also clear, as Steers (1977) has pointed out, is that the quality of an organization's climate is directly related to the degree of **organizational effectiveness.**

(e) Steers has offered a 'process model' of the 'dynamics of effectiveness in on-going organizations'. In doing so, he tries to marry a 'systems' perspective with an emphasis on the human side of the enterprise by arguing that the **process of exchange** is crucial within an effective organization:

> Every member may not value all the objectives equally; instead, an individual would probably pursue some less valued (to him) goals in exchange for securing the efforts of others on those goals that are more highly valued by him. Thus, through coalition and cooperation, members of an organization attempt to satisfy their diverse needs and goals to the extent (that is) commensurate with resources.

He contends that there is an exchange relationship between personal and organizational (i.e. shared) goals and that individuals will participate in organizational activities to the extent that the rewards are commensurate with their efforts. Thus, to him, 'goals' are the manifestations of motives or 'needs'. And the formulation of shared goals for an organization is the process of exchange in action. Shared goals — the 'product' of this process — serve to:

focus attention;
provide direction;
legitimate certain agendas;
establish a rationale for organizing activities, practices and processes;
provide standards of assessment;
provide legitimacy in the eyes of various audiences or groups;
concentrate the allocation of resources.

In other words, through goal-setting according to the exchange model, Steers provides a more systematic approach involving more human considerations in order to achieve organizational effectiveness.

(f) The capacity to operate as a Learning School is a vital pre-condition for growth and development. School readiness is a key element in school development. And 'readiness' is linked to:

the preparedness to investigate performance gaps;
the recognition of the need to change;
the establishment of a proper climate for change;
the acquisition of the tools to diagnose the nature of the problem;
the capacity to launch into development work.

Three points are pertinent here:

(i) 'Pre-conditions' can be established *during* the development work. They may take the form of process outcomes. In other words, the absence of pre-conditions *initially* should not be used as a reason for postponing the doing of development.
(ii) Nevertheless, it has been discovered that the condition of the school on entry to a programme of development will to a large extent determine the level of success achieved. It seems that schools succeed in going forward according to their capacity to go forward (see Miller, 1988).
(iii) Moreover, an important pre-condition for growth is the quality of the school's leadership.

Level 5: Leadership for learning

Everyone agrees that the quality of leadership exercised by the head teacher is crucial for the Learning School. He or she can set the tone for learning (by children and adults alike) and can model the behaviour necessary for learning. The headteacher, therefore, is the leading learner. He/she can be a learner (and talk openly about the process to others) and can facilitate and support the learning of others.

In addition, more than anyone else, the headteacher can 'walk the climate of learning' (in terms of **modelling** learning, **being** a learner and **manifesting** it).

According to Bennis and Nanus (1985), leadership is vital for organizational learning:

> . . . some organizations (are) more effective than others at innovative learning. The difference is **leadership,** without which organizational learning is unfocused — lacking in energy, force, cohesion, and purpose.

The same authors are in agreement with our stance when they maintain that school leaders need to be enthusiastic learners themselves (in terms of being open to new experiences and seeking new challenges and opportunities for self-improvement), while stimulating learning in others by serving as a role model. Such behaviour should include:

encouraging risk-taking;
displaying the capacity to listen and to be taught;
rewarding the learning of others;
creating a conducive climate for learning.

Bennis and Nanus (1985) usefully differentiate between **maintenance learning** (the acquisition of methods, routines and the wherewithal to learn how to operate in a problem-solving mode to maintain the existing system) and **innovative learning** (involving renewal, restructuring and problem reformulation). They argue that innovative learning is more difficult because it focusses on the preparation of organizations for new action in new situations; it requires anticipation of the — as yet — unknown. Moreover, they contend, there are six modes of innovative learning:

reinterpretation of history: redefining traditions in the light of the new reality;
experimentation: testing hypotheses about the direction of change — by feel and feedback. They call it 'groping into the future';

analagous organizations: observing the experiences of other similar organizations and indulging in what Peters (1987) has called 'creative swiping';
analytical processes: the conscious process of analyzing trends in the external environment and identifying the emerging issues;
training and education: formal opportunities for learning;
unlearning: discarding old 'learnings'.

Handy (1987) has also explored the nature of 'discontinuous' learning, which he refers to as 'inverted doughnut thinking' (i.e. embarking on an exploration from the security of the solid core to the insecurity of the space around), and has concluded that **change** and **learning** are linked by **encouragement.** He agrees with Bennis and Nanus when he says that it is a question of learning to behave like a scientist — asking questions, seeking possible answers, testing possibilities, i.e. trial and error learning. Handy concludes that:

> . . . under conditions of discontinuity we all will have to learn to live with bigger doughnuts, with more space. It is that sort of learning with which I am concerned, because, ironically, under the pressure of uncertainty most people and institutions instinctively do the opposite, they creep back to the core . . . If we as individuals and we as a society are going to enjoy the opportunities offered by discontinuous change we must become more used to venturing into the spaces of the doughnut, become more experimental, more tolerant of failure, more ambitious in our aims, more self-confident, more flexible and more cooperative.

Above all, says Handy, such learning needs **encouragers;** 'mentors' are required to instil self-confidence, promote creative thinking, recognize achievement, provide support and give counsel in failure. These are all leadership tasks. And more recently, in a challenging 'thought-piece' entitled 'What's worth fighting for in the principalship?', Fullan (1988) has described the central task of empowered managers — 'perpetual learning'. He concludes that,

> when it comes to learning, effective leaders are greedy . . . The advice for principals, in a nutshell, is to get into the habit of and situations for constant learning.

Holly (1989) has incorporated the point made by Fullan (1986) — that effective change is initiated and sustained by a combination of pressure and support — and the two sides of the leadership equation, the initiating structure and consideration, with the four dimensions of change in schools as indentified by Charters and Jones (1973), into the following diagram:

Figure 3: Management for change

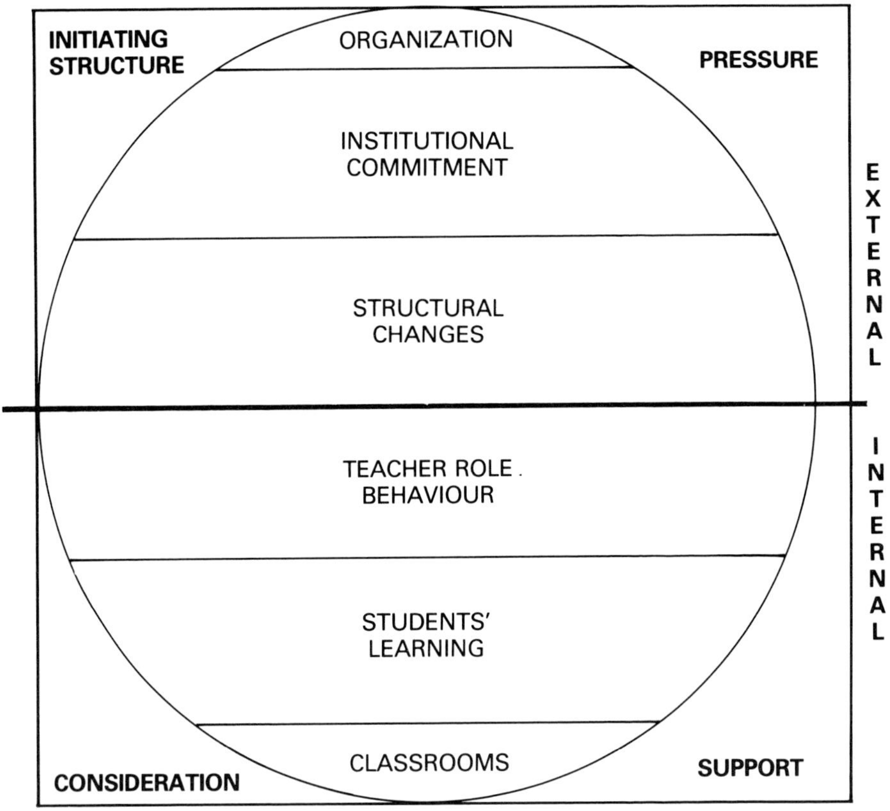

His stance is that the **external curriculum** (external, that is, to the classroom) is composed of institutional commitment and structural changes and provides both pressure and support/the initiating structure and consideration for the **internal curriculum,** i.e. the classroom dimension. Leadership for learning is manifested within the external curriculum in order to influence the nature of the action within the internal curriculum. The Learning School, therefore, encompasses both these dimensions.

Extending this point, we would argue that the headteacher as the leading learner in the organization has two vital contributions to make towards the creation of the Learning School:

1 Headteachers must do everything possible to prevent the 'bureaucratization' of their schools.

According to McNeil (1988), schools are often in conflict with themselves. They aim to enhance learning and end up organizing it out of existence. In other words by focussing on the coherence of the school as an organization, the staff can unwittingly undermine and displace their central goal — the advancement of teaching and learning. As McNeil argues:

> The traditional justification for the bureaucratic organization of schools has been that a smooth-running school facilitates learning. But when the attention to 'smooth-running' begins to control the educational practice in a school, teachers react in ways that reduce educational quality rather than enhance it. **In fact, teachers tend to control their students in much the same way as they are controlled by administrators . . .** The ritual of seeming to deal with a topic (can be) more important than actually teaching and learning it.

Holly (1983) has referred to the LCD mentality in schools and the fact that this 'pathology' endangers the quality of children's learning. And McNeil contends that this mentality is partly caused by the separation of the domains of teaching and administration. Yet, she says,

> in those schools that make educational goals the top priority and arrange administrative policies to serve educational ends rather than order-keeping . . . teachers are more likely to feel secure enough to take risks, to go on learning along with their students, and, most important, to bring their richest and most complicated knowledge of their subjects into their courses.

Consequently, the school as a learning organization must put the priorities of **learning** before the demands of the **organization.** Moreover, the headteacher, as the leading organizer, needs to retain the spirit of the leading learner; and, as we have mentioned above, the Learning School needs to be 'managed' like a good classroom, i.e. for the enhancement of learning.

2 Headteachers must lead the attempt to transform the Learning School into its dynamic version, the Developing School.

Dalin and Rust (1983) have posed the vital question — 'Can Schools Learn?' Their response is a positive one. Given certain conditions, they argue, schools can learn and develop from the inside. Indeed, one of these 'conditions' is that the school is acknowledged as the key educational unit and the basic unit for educational development and improvement. The staff members then become the energy source for development. 'Genuine school renewal,' they say,

> requires that those actually living and working in the school be directly involved in defining needs, setting goals, and participating in programme development.

According to Dalin and Rust, there are three sides to the equation of school-based development:

- The first is the **internal creativity of the school.** They refer to the definition of the 'Creative School' suggested by Nisbet (1974), i.e. it is a school with the **capacity to adopt, adapt, generate or reject innovations.** Dalin and Rust extend this definition when they say that such a school has to have the desire and capacity to thoroughly self-evaluate the values, the structures, the relationships and the strategies for action prevalent within the school, plus the capacity to use this information as the basis for planning, implementation and evaluation of the changes. These are the properties, they say, of the problem-solving school.
- The second is the **capacity of the school to respond to environmental pressures** (whether they arise from political, social, economic, technical or cultural sources) in as productive a manner as possible.
- The third is the vital interaction between the internally motivated designs of the school and the environmental pressures mentioned above. This process of integration and accommodation is referred to by Dalin and Rust as **mutual adaptation.**

Taken together, these three points tell us much about the process of school-based development. While it is an internal process, it is not an introverted one. The school's learning — the basis of the development work — arises from a partnership of resolve, involving partners from both inside and outside the school. The Developing School, therefore, is linked with its external world by means of this learning partnership, through which it becomes aware of, and responsive to, the nature of external demands. As Dalin and Rust (1983) conclude:

> The most productive innovation climate involves a **dialogue** between the school and its environment.

Indeed, more recently, Dalin (1988) has outlined the following conditions for school-based development:

- consider the individual school as the unit of change;
- provide support for risk-taking and the introduction of innovative practices;
- take a long-term perspective;
- avoid the 'bureaucratic kiss of death';
- think in 'dramatically new ways';
- explore the central dilemma of 'managing' and organizing an innovative programme;
- consider the management of the complexities of the change process;
- be flexible and enable each school involved to become a 'unique educational system';
- encourage differentiation and decentralization;
- assist forward-looking 'change agents' and support their learning.

Key concepts for the Learning School (as, indeed, for the Developing School) emerge from the lexicon of learning.

The Learning School aims to be like learning itself:

interactive and negotiative:
creative and problem-solving;
proactive and responsive;
participative and collaborative;
flexible and challenging;
risk-taking and enterprising;
evaluative and reflective;
supportive and developmental.

Chapter 2

The Developing School

When **the Learning School** is activated by means of various developmental processes, it becomes **the Developing School.**

Other commentators have referred to:

the Thinking School;
the Creative School;
the Problem-Solving School;
the Evaluative School.

The Developing School is all these things and more. Its distinctive quality lies in its capacity to move forward effectively and according to a particular style, a 'house-style'. It is a question of generating the common understanding across the staff that this is the way we go forward in this school. Holly (in Reid, Hopkins and Holly, 1987) has referred to this organic approach as a school's **development culture.**

The Development Culture

In our view there are four elements in a school's development culture. These elements constitute key understandings which need to be shared across the staff of the Developing School. It is very much a case of:

1 Development as Opposed to Innovation

As Holly (1985) has remarked, 'while innovations are (to be) carefully introduced, innovation is not the order of the day, development is'.

While development begins in the present, it is rooted in past achievements.

It is also a case of the internal generation of change initiatives as opposed to their external imposition. As Goodlad (1987) has argued:

> Schools will improve slowly, if at all, if reforms are thrust upon them. Rather, the approach having most promise, in my judgment, is one that will seek to **cultivate the capacity** of schools to deal with their own problems, to become largely self-renewing.

In stressing the need to nurture the growth of an internal capacity for school renewal, Goodlad is not denying the importance of the external environment. Indeed, Goodlad (*ibid*) has since provided an ecological interpretation of school renewal. In other words, a forward-looking and forward-moving school must do so in dialogue with the demands and pressures arising from the external environment. But the school which is exercising responsible autonomy in these matters must retain power of attorney. Innovation overload is the chief enemy of the Developing School, the reason, according to a headline in the *Times Educational Supplement,* 'why the foot-soldiers have become bogged down'. As Fullan (1988) has contended recently, the overload arising from multiple initiatives leads to dependency not enterprise. An enterprising school must have the power to sift through the innovations vying for its attention and decide which of them represents what the members of staff actually need at this point in time. Ordering priorities is a central activity within a development culture. We think that Naisbitt (1984) has summed up some of these issues rather well:

> Change that bubbles up from the grassroots has staying power . . . For best results, the people in the institution must have **ownership** in the new vision . . . decisions will be made from the bottom-up in a participatory fashion rather than top-down. **Re-thinking** (is) a constant, long-term process . . . the word process should be emphasized . . . (It) is not a product you get or bring in from the outside. It is something that occurs inside an institution (**but well instructed by what is going on outside**). And it must be a shared vision, a strategic vision.

As we said in chapter 1, the Learning School is the Listening School. In terms of its developmental decisions, it is tutored by, but not dependent upon, the messages arising from its external world. The relationship is a learning one.

School development grows from the inside, tempered by what is happening on the outside.

2 *Evolution as Opposed to Revolution*

It involves the gradual unfolding of growth. Change in the Developing School tends to be incremental, until, as Handy (1987) has recently pointed out, so much progress will have been made that there will be a more rapid 'flip' and more radical change will occur. Handy refers to this eventuality as 'discontinuous incrementalism'. It is worth emphasizing, however, that this stage is only reached after much steady, more continuous growth. Evolutionary growth is the norm. Naisbitt (1984) has referred to the process of innovation in similar terms. He outlined three stages in the process: the first involves taking the 'path of least resistance' so as not to threaten people and thus reduce the 'chances of abrupt rejection'; the second entails using the new ideas to improve what we already have; and the third can often mean the pursuit of new directions which, originally, cannot be foreseen. The important point, however, is that, particularly during the early days of the change process, continuity, synthesis (of the best of the old with the best of the new) and incrementalism are vital factors.

3 *Systematic Endeavour as Opposed to the Pursuit of the Idiosyncratic*

Development, according to its dictionary definition, involves bringing out the full potential of the school as an organization, which entails bringing it to a more advanced, highly organized state. Accordingly, school development becomes an advance through successive stages, a spiral of growth. It is also a way of life; *the* way to move forward. This systematic, thorough approach involves the fusion of various kinds of endeavour.

The Developing School, as described in this volume, is a model for advancement. We would argue, however, that this is not a linear or mechanistic model. The emphasis on being systematic (i.e. being determined, resolved, resourceful and integrated in pursuit of a vision) can be set against the willingness to be opportunistic, piecemeal and strategic in the doing of it. The Developing School lives the tensions between systematic and non-systematic approaches, between the rational and the non-rational and between organizational and more individualistic orientations and, in so doing, resolves the tensions in as productive a manner as possible.

As Holly (1985) has argued, school development is a 'package deal' involving the integration of various 'building-blocks'. As Goodlad

(1987) maintained,

> Efforts at improvement must encompass the school as a system of interacting parts, each affecting the others.

Three of these interacting points are:

(a) **Management development**
Into the future, stronger and more independent schools will need stronger leadership (see Goodchild and Holly, 1989).

(b) **Staff development**
And these stronger schools will need stronger staffs. These staff members will need to become enhanced professionals, professionally-driven and professionally-accountable. They will also need to work in concert. The Developing School is built on the firm foundations of staff professionalism and staff collaboration. The emphasis will no longer be on acquisitive, competitive individualism; it will no longer be good enough to entertain 'over-developed individuals in under-developed schools' (see Reid, Hopkins and Holly, 1987). Staff members will need to work together to build *their* school. As Fenstermacher and Berliner (1985) have remarked, staff development now:

> is not the same as the in-service education of earlier decades. In earlier times, teachers were typically thought to have the primary responsibility for their own renewal, reading what they believed most helpful, taking such courses as they thought valuable for their work, and attending clinics and workshops that promised to increase their capacity to instruct. It is no longer possible for teachers to close their classroom doors and, in doing so, disconnect themselves from the world beyond . . . staff development has become an activity that encompasses much more than a single teacher acting as an individual; it is understood that this person's activities are a part of the larger environment of the school. Modern staff development is an enterprise of groups of teachers, often working in concert with specialists, supervisors, school administrators, counsellors, parents, and many other people who populate, or are connected with, the modern school. As such, staff development has become a major activity, involving the time and resources of many people and making extensive demands on school system budgets.

Individual members of staff are vital within the Developing School, but their ability to work in collaboration is more vital.

(c) **Curriculum development**
The focus will be on a stronger, more cohesive curriculum which is implemented with panache at the classroom level.

4 Internal as Opposed to External Evaluation

And the process of fusion is triggered, we would suggest, by staff involvement in self-evaluation, i.e. **collaborative enquiry.**

Figure 4:

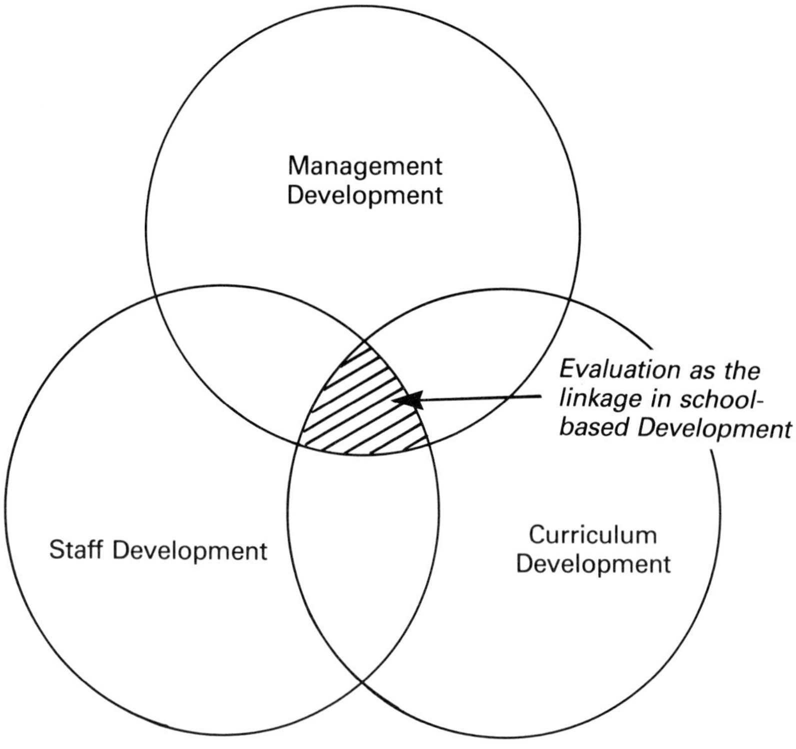

Self-evaluation provides the necessary linkage, indeed the life-blood, of the Developing School. It is the vehicle for growth and development; it provides the motive energy. Holly (1985) has produced a process framework for school development which hinges around five different approaches to evaluation (see Figure 5, page 30). Moreover, this schema, in large part, integrates evaluation within a planning process. It provides the substance for a **School Development Plan.**

The process of producing a School Development Plan is now a well established practice derived from several roots:

(a) The shift towards the wider involvement of staff in school-focussed INSET and staff development initiatives

> We have not invented the concept of school development. It has operated for many years in a few schools, though very often the process has been implicit rather than explicit. It has been stimulated by the ILEA's scheme for funding school-focussed INSET, begun in 1980. The shift of emphasis proposed here is to strengthen the trend towards developing schools rather than individual teachers, with the bulk of the in-service education for teachers being conducted at school level and, wherever it is conducted, being aimed at whole school improvement; **the benefit to the individual teacher is important but secondary.** (From *Improving Primary Schools,* ILEA's Report of the Committee on Primary Education, 1985.)

(b) The shift to an emphasis on corporate, school-based development. Again, this trend was noted in ILEA's 'Thomas Report':

> . . . If the whole school is to benefit and the improvement to be consolidated, a clear and preferably corporate view has to be formed about the school's strengths and weaknesses . . . and what subsequent action will be required inside the school . . . They (the schools) should set up arrangements to review where they are in relation to the many aspects of their internal and external environment, and to make plans for working on some of them.

(c) The introduction of 'GRIST' (Grant-Related In-Service Training) accelerated the shift to schools holding their own INSET funds and the concomitant demands for negotiated needs-based provision and, therefore, internal accountability.

(d) The accumulated experience of operating schemes for school self-evaluation. With the increasing emphasis on process frameworks (for example, the GRIDS scheme), school self-evaluation has become synonymous with school-based development.

(e) The growing awareness that INSET is not an independent activity; that it can be a service operation in support of the implementation of measured innovation. This fusion process (as described above) helps staff members to have a purchase on the change process. By concentrating on

key areas of focus, sustained movement becomes a possibility and INSET needs can be planned with more precision.

Hargreaves (1988), in reflecting on his ILEA experience with School Development Plans, has suggested the practical scheme given in figure 5. While we are more used to using the GRIDS approach (and its amended format — see 'The Teachers' GUIDE' compiled by Holly,

Figure 5:

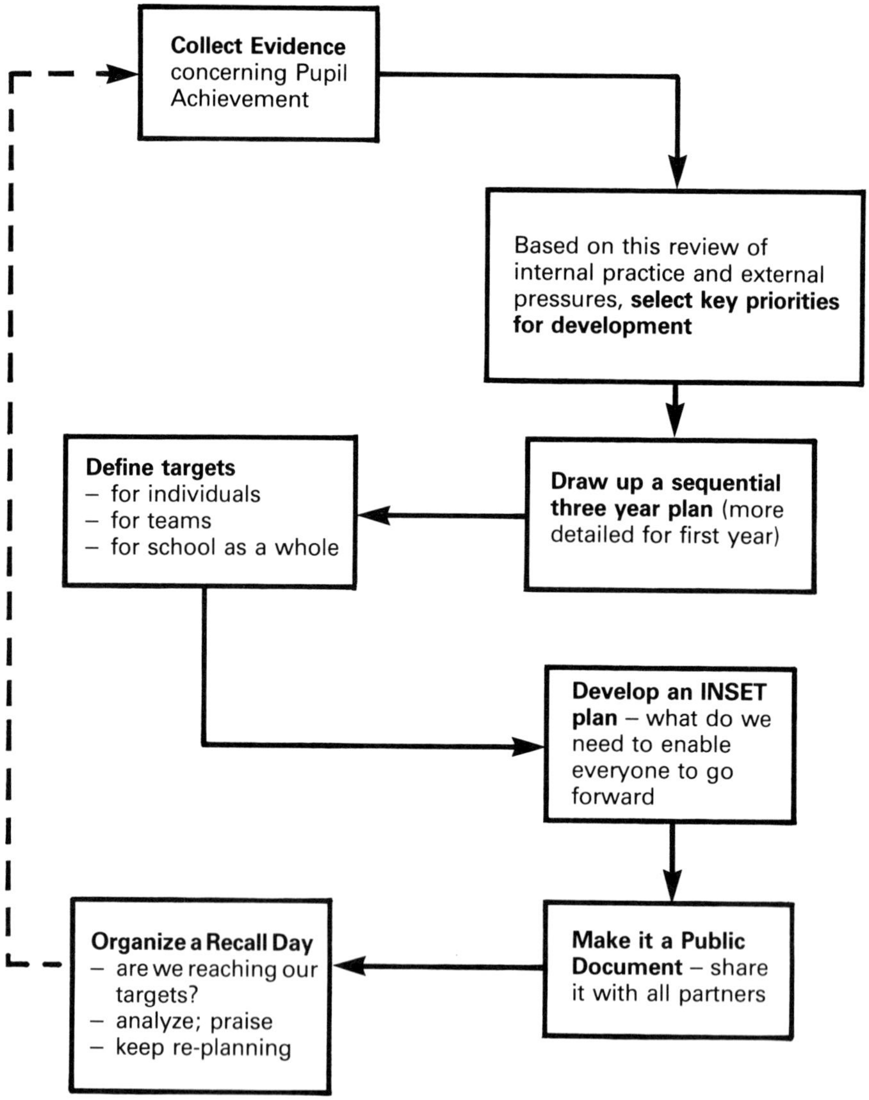

1986c) as a process framework, we can see great potential in this particular model. While there are many similarities between the two approaches, there is one interesting difference. Whereas the GRIDS scheme encourages a review of current practice in the prioritized 'key area of focus', in the ILEA scheme, the priorities for development emerge from a more general review of practice across the school. We consider it most important that each school finds its own conducive framework. What are important are the processes themselves, not the precise assemblage of them. Having argued for procedural flexibility, we would recommend that every school should become involved in the process of formulating a School Development Plan.

School Development Plans

We now introduce a key feature of school development, it is that each school formulates, records and utilizes a *development plan*. The idea of school development plans was first raised to prominence by the ILEA's Report of the Committee on Primary Education (ILEA, 1985) which said:

> We recommend that every school should have a plan for development, taking account of the policies of the LEA, the needs of the children, the capacities of the staff and the known views of the parents. The plan should have an action sheet attached to it showing what the responsibilities of members of staff will be and setting target dates. The plan should also show what, if any, outside assistance or special resources will be needed and indicate timescales; it should also show by what means the effects of the plan are to be assessed. The central purpose should be expressed in terms of the improvements sought in the children's learning.

The ILEA Report acknowledged that the concept of school development was not new and had operated for many years in a number of schools though often the process had been implicit rather than explicit (para.3.89). Development plans were further promoted when the House of Commons Select Committee (1986), said:

> We recommend that all primary schools should be required to operate according to development plans agreed with the governing body and LEA . . . We believe that such a requirement would provide a good opportunity for heads and teachers to use their initiative and imagination; to influence the

> form and content of INSET so that it relates directly to the children's needs and their needs; and that the arrangement would disallow stagnation and lethargy. The plan should be a whole school plan to which all teachers should contribute as class teachers and, to a greater or lesser degree, as co-ordinators; it should act as a unifying force in the work of staff and children.

It can be seen from both of these recommendations, and the discussions in the reports that prefaced them, that a number of characteristics are involved. Campbell (1987) has identified some of the characteristics and drawing on her work we will set them out and discuss them in turn.

Characteristics of School Development Plans

1 *A belief that the development of schools grows from within*
Underlying the recommendations made by the House of Commons Select Committee and the ILEA Report is the belief that a school's development is the responsibility of those who work within it:

> We believe that we have now reached one of the most crucial points in this Report. It is that the development of schools grows from within and that they should work continuously and actively towards their own improvement. (ILEA, 1985)

This view is in harmony with our own view of school development (see chapter 1) and the prevailing attitudes of heads since heads expect to set their school's philosophy (see chapter 3) and appear to be the leading agents of change (see Nias *et al* 1989; Southworth and Myer, 1988). Moreover, it makes sense for schools to grow and develop from where they are. First, each school's individual circumstances need to be taken into account. Just as leadership is, in part, contingent upon the school's context, so too is the school's development. If a school has recently had a high turnover of staff, or just completed a major review of language development then each of these could affect the school's next area of development and needs to be borne in mind. Second, it is a truism that schools can only develop from where they are. Quite often we know where we want to go but wish we did not have to start from here — alas we do! Growing from within is therefore about development based on reality — where we are.

There are three other reasons for schools growing from within. The first of these is that of 'ownership'. Staff feel more in control and committed to developments they are involved with and responsible for. Second, school development, can in one sense, only be internal. For sure, 'outsiders' can be involved, offer support, and help to set the agenda of change, but ultimately development rests upon teachers in classrooms, ancillary staff around the school, and the headteacher in the school all working to make developments happen. Without their involvement, very little else will change. Third, much growth has come from using and spreading the talents of those working in the school. Teachers do not only teach children, teachers can teach teachers! Many teachers developed because they learned from their colleagues within their own schools (see Southworth, 1984) and development plans should clearly continue this well known and valuable form of school and teacher development.

2 *The plan should be a whole school plan*

Teachers should be consulted and involved in devising the plan. The ILEA Report believed that it was a matter of high priority that each school should have a sense of wholeness and that can be achieved only through clear and sensitive leadership and after the adjustments that inevitably follow staff discussions arranged to consider proposals. Further:

> We have noticed that morale is invariably high in schools where there is a strongly developed corporate view on the ways in which they should develop. . . . though we realize that its attainment is not always easy . . . we wish only to add that a regular programme of curricular meetings seems often to be an important element in development cohesion and can, when well conducted, help members of staff to support each other in what may be painful self-examination. (ILEA, 1985)

Schools might take advantage of GRIST and the now mandatory in-service days (or sessions) to develop a sense of cohesion by engaging in team-building work (see, for example, Eason, 1985). In other words, one aspect of a development plan might be to develop the staff's teamwork.

Whether the plan intentionally or unintentionally aims to develop teamwork, it is clear that school development plans might be vehicles for unifying the work of staff and children. If so they might contribute positively to the development of a whole school approach which many see as valuable and necessary (see Thomas, 1987; Campbell, 1985; Southworth, 1987). In other words the plan brings together the views, ideas and aspirations of all members of the school's staff and becomes the way forward for all of them. Thus, not only does the plan bring ideas together but it also becomes the staff's collective view of how and where the school should be developing.

3 *Consideration of the views of the LEA and central government*
Whilst development should grow from within this could be rather narrowing in terms of educational perspectives. Also, it might be risky (or even unprofessional) to ignore the views of the LEA. This might apply in respect of LEA school reviews, inspections, the policies of the Education Committee and the work of the LEA advisers/inspectors. Moreover, schools clearly need to be aware of legislation; for example, legislation pertaining to equal opportunities (in respect of race, gender and disability). Schools also need to reflect LEA guidelines and adhere to them.

With the advent of the 'National Curriculum' schools will also need to take account of developments at national level (for example, assessment, subject working party reports and update work) and, of course, those arising from national legislation (for example, the 1980, 1981 and 1986 Education Acts). Whilst schools should develop from within they need to be fully aware of, and alert to, the ideas and wishes of others who have a stake in school development. Schools, like many other organizations, can become 'inside focussed'. That is, they become preoccupied with internal matters and machinations and begin to lose sight of developments outside the school. Also, the changes and turbulence which schools faced in the 1980s, and will continue to face in the 1990s, can develop a siege mentality where it is easier and safer to 'pull up the drawbridge' and concentrate purely on the day-to-day business of the school and try to forget about the external changes and challenges. Those inside schools who wish to develop their schools now need to be much more concerned with the views of those outside schools. Schools should become both inside and outside focussed.

4 *Consideration of the known views of parents*
Many headteachers are keenly aware of 'their' schools' reputation and image, and are alert to parental views. However, the perceptions of heads might be both partial and unrepresentative if they spend a good deal of their parental time in contact with, say, critical or disaffected parents, or alternatively, parents who are well satisfied with their children's success. Maybe such groups are vocal minorities? Clearly the issue here is for schools to try to discover the views of a cross-section of parents, if not a representative sample.

The introduction of an annual parents' meeting could prove a useful forum. Also, parental governors might play an important role in gathering the views of parents. Moreover, in addition to gathering in views, such contacts could also assist in disseminating the development work of the school and in fostering a supportive external context for internal development.

5 *Agreeing the plan with governors*
It is both necessary and prudent to secure the agreement, indeed, support of governors to the school's plan. It may be that some schools will seek to involve governors in the process of putting the plan together (for example, parent governors, teacher and staff representatives). In particular we would recommend that chairpersons should be kept fully informed and, wherever possible, involved.

Links have already been suggested between considering the known views of parents and governors through the parent governors' role. Other links could be developed at the annual parents' meetings when, hopefully, governors might not only present the school's development plan as something jointly agreed but as wholeheartedly approved and endorsed. This could be an important message to parents. Moreover, if a tripartite agreement is secured between school, governors and parents then mutual understanding and confidence will grow and will surely enhance the school's development and the management of change.

Indeed, consideration of the views of the LEA, parents and governors is crucial to the successful management of change. As Fullan (1985) says, there are some horror stories of what happens if the community is ignored when major innovations are introduced and the best advice seems to be that, at a minimum, schools 'should be wary that parents and the community are not opposed to an innovation. At a maximum, they should involve parents (and we would add governors) in planning and in supportive roles in relation to an innovation'.

6 *The plan should be derived from a review of current practice*
Schools '. . . should set up arrangements to review where they are in relation to the many aspects of their internal and external environment' (ILEA, 1985, para 3.88). This characteristic is consistent with our position on evaluation for development (see chapter 5). It is also in accord with the school self evaluation movement which was active in the early 1980s and in many cases still is. Several LEAs either mandated, or advised, schools to undertake reviews and many useful guidelines were produced (see Salford, Suffolk, Lancashire, ILEA, Oxford). Also, the adoption in many schools of GRIDS (Guidelines for the Review of Internal Developments in Schools; Schools Council Programme 1) provides an alternative approach.

Campbell (1987) having identified a number of the characteristics of school development plans then visited eight schools which were utilizing development plans. She found that a:

> review of some kind had evidently been part of the process of drawing up the development plan in all the schools I visited. In

> one case a formal review was carried out by the LEA over a period of a week and as a result action groups were established within the school to consider specific aspects of the school's organization and practice. Some schools used GRIDS as a basic starting point, though in one case this was adapted and in another discarded. Other schools used questionnaires. The advantages of this method were that it canvassed the views of all the staff, not only those who were prepared to speak in staff meetings; it was designed with the particular school in mind; it was relatively quick and easy for staff to complete (though not, I suspect, to design) and the results could be used as a basis for staff discussion about the development plan. In one school such discussion took place as a whole staff group. In another school discussion was between individual staff members and the INSET coordinator — a very time-consuming process that was nevertheless felt to be worthwhile.
>
> The purpose of the review in each case was to identify the needs of the school. In some cases these reflected what one headteacher saw as the inevitable concern of primary school teachers with language and mathematics and these concerns seemed most likely to be expressed in terms of pupil achievement. Other concerns, such as that for science, seemed to reflect uncertainties among staff about their own confidence and expertise.

In such a way the needs and concerns of staff might begin to be identified. However, one could go further since 'staff' need not only apply to teaching staff. The needs of ancillary staff are important. Nursery nurses, welfare assistants and ancillary workers all have important dealings and conversations with children and influence the child's curriculum. Schools should not overlook the needs of these members of staff, nor their development. If the notion of a 'whole' school is to have any currency then ancillary and other staff need to be regarded as active and valued members of the school and its development.

Nor too should the needs of the children be omitted. The majority of schools would claim that their plans are intended to improve the educational provision for the children. However, a review should seek for *evidence* rather than rhetoric. Therefore, reviews should look closely at the received curriculum, and children's work as process and product. And this will be particularly true as schools move into their second cycle of drafting school development plans because these should be based upon a review of the first development plan and its implementation and success in terms of the children's activities.

Reviews should help to avoid lethargy and inertia in the school by countering any tendencies to stagnation (although many teachers might feel that during the 1980s schools have hardly been stagnant). The assumption here is that discussions arising from the review will be stimulating and increase awareness. However, this might prove optimistic since there is no guarantee that a review will, by itself, penetrate complacency or unquestioning self-satisfaction. Perhaps some reviews might involve a 'critical friend', LEA inspector/adviser, or some person external to the school who could offer an alternative viewpoint?

If schools *are* to grow from within then (as item 1 mentions) schools need to know where they are. Reviews should provide a better view of where we are; hence they are a necessary step in the process of growing and developing.

7 *Priorities*

Having identified the needs of the school in the light of children's, staff's, parents', governors', and LEA and central government's policies and wishes, priorities might then have to be established.

Priorities will be determined by each school, and will therefore be tailored in accordance with the perceived circumstances, preferences and requirements of the school as a whole. Deciding priorities may be a sensitive process and one where heads in particular may need to exercise judicial skill and diplomacy. However, whilst priorities are sensible they can sometimes be seen as too rigid and sequential. Since schools have to simultaneously respond to multiple demands (for example, central government, community, LEA, professional associations and unions) and deal with proposals from groups which may not be homogeneous (for example, parents, governors, community), it is not surprising that schools can face incompatible or conflicting requests and expectations. Moreover, any or all of these may change rather suddenly (for example, recall the speed with which government in 1987 moved to drafting the 1988 Education Act). In short, schools operate within turbulent environments and prioritizing needs to offer some focus and certainty but in such a way that the school is not wholly locked onto the plan: some flexibility is needed.

One possible way forward is for each school to try to ensure it does not attempt too ambitious a plan whereby the school is saturated in developments to the point that nothing else can be absorbed. Schools will vary in the number of developments they feel able to undertake. Schools might also vary the number of priorities from year to year. It might be the case that different priorities are different in scale (for example, mathematics across the curriculum compared to introducing large play apparatus for the reception infants class). It is also likely that some priorities will arise from LEA policies and priorities. Nevertheless, having a plan should help schools to be selective about the issues they feel ready to face and resolve.

Another feature of prioritizing is that an action points sheet is produced and, we would add, that it is 'published' to all interested parties. The action points sheet is a list of things to be done. It will set out what the school has decided to develop. Schools might also need to express these in some detail and with some clarity (see points 8 and 9). The action points translate the priorities into targets.

8 *The central purpose should be expressed in terms of the improvements sought in the children's learning*

Chapter 4 suggests that one feature of curriculum coordinators and their part in curriculum development in the past was the tendency for there to be no *direct* connection between their advice and support to colleagues, and changes in classroom practice and the children's learning (see p. 70). A school development plan should make that connection because the plan should record, at the start of the plan's implementation, the improvements sought in the children's learning.

While this seems logical and obvious the absence of precedents on anything like a large scale makes this characteristic rather novel and demanding. Yet, it is vital that staff 'think through' proposals for development and try to anticipate what these developments will look like in classrooms, in the children's activities and in their learning.

For example, in changing a mathematics scheme what is it one expects the new scheme to develop? Greater interest in mathematics? Increased problem-solving activities? More investigational activities? Greater cooperation and group work? Cross-curricular links? It is important that these kinds of thoughts are captured by the staff as a whole, shared, refined and sharpened. It is likely to be an easier task if all staff contribute to it rather than, say, leaving it to an individual curriculum coordinator (for example, the maths coordinator in this example). Such a task could be rather daunting for an individual. Moreover, it is necessary to ensure a whole school perspective, and it is also important that those who teach the older children are aware of the expectations of those who teach the younger children (and vice versa).

In setting down expectations for improvement staff will be engaged upon an intensely practical task, and an absolutely central one since they are not only mapping out in detail the anticipated improvements in the children's learning, but also compiling the criteria for judging the success of the development plan. If, after some agreed passage of time, those changes have not occurred, then serious questions and doubts will be raised about the developments. Of course, evaluation of the children's learning will be needed and this may take a variety of forms (for example, teacher perceptions, subjective judgments, observation of children, pupil records, diagnostic tests, examples of children's work), indeed a host of approaches could be applied, but criteria for judging the success of the plan are needed and these should be determined at the outset, and expressed in terms of improvements sought in the children's learning.

9 *Time schedules*

The plan should indicate time schedules. Target dates should be set and everyone should be aware of them. 'A plan might well take more than a year; and would be one of a continuing series' (House of Commons Select Committee, 1986, para 13.14). It might be the case that 'within' a school's plan target dates for different developments vary (for example, handwriting policy adopted within one term; all classes to undertake educational visits to aspects of local community within two terms).

It is also possible that schools prepare a plan for, say, three years, only the first year of which is prepared in detail with the other two years outlined. Then, as those years are approached they are updated and planned in greater detail.

The plan might be thought of as a calendar. In addition to start and completion dates, key events could be timetabled (for example, visit by outside speaker; INSET activities; meetings; visits to colleagues' classrooms; workshops; exhibitions, parent and governor involvements).

10 *Identification of outside help*

Increasingly there are LEA support staff available to help schools. Some of these staff operate as teams, others as individuals. Often they are advisory teachers. They vary from LEA to LEA in terms of the curricular issues and areas they focus on but it is common for a single LEA to offer support in respect of: multicultural education, under-5s, mathematics, special needs, reading, computers and INSET planning.

Additionally there might be colleagues in neighbouring schools who have expertise in the school's priority areas, or the school might approach LEA advisers/inspectors, teacher centres and higher education establishments. Lastly, there is usually some provision for in-service which the school might build into its plan.

Obviously, it makes sense for schools to draw upon the experience of others and some time should be devoted to considering who, if anyone, might be available to the school.

11 *Analyze resource implications*

The ILEA Report made it clear that in devising a development plan the school should be aware of the availability of resources within the LEA. The House of Commons Select Committee said: 'The plan should indicate any major shift required in the provision of books or other resources' (para 3.16). This is a relatively straightforward task. Moreover, perhaps some kind of budgetting will be needed in order to provide some financial support for the plan, if required. Such decisions should be made in the light of the plan, and should be communicated to all staff and agreed. Since primary schools are not centres of wealth and capital (!) they have to husband their resources with great care. Budgetting and planning are therefore essential and the opportunity to combine and *synchronize* them should be regarded as a benefit to the school's management.

However, money is only one kind of resource and a more generous definition of resources should be adopted. For example, maybe an internal redistribution of curriculum materials could be undertaken, or perhaps, instead of continuing to purchase one kind of material a change is needed (for example, different sets of books, worksheets, kits, art materials).

Time might also be analyzed. Perhaps ancillary staff, or the headteacher, will need to readjust the scheduling and periods of time they traditionally, or currently, have devoted to certain tasks, classes or colleagues. If a particularly heavy burden falls upon an individual teacher because of the plan's agreed priorities then it might be sensible to offer that teacher additional support (ancillary, secretarial), extra funding, and/or some release from class teaching.

One important resource implication will be in respect of teacher development, and INSET. Since many schools are now involved, through GRIST arrangements, in managing the identification of in-service needs and in providing for them, then schools will find it useful to connect these plans to those for school development. For example, if the school development plan puts a priority on environmental studies, then in addition to purchasing resources, and locating environmental study resources and expertise in the LEA, it would be sensible to devote INSET funds to certain staff who would benefit from an in-service course or experience in environmental studies. Also, the school might undertake a school-based workshop or conference, bringing in LEA staff or an INSET provider.

12 *Contractual nature of school development plans*

The ILEA Committee on Primary Education (1985) conceived school development plans as providing growth from within. However, although internal plans establish ownership and help staff to feel in control schools need to be accountable to others outside the school, as characteristics 3, 4 and 5 suggest. Those characteristics spoke of securing the agreement of the LEA, parents and governors, and in the light of the 1986 and 1988

Education Acts this is now an imperative. Yet the ILEA (1985) took the idea of agreement one step further:

> Agreement on the plan by the school, governors and the divisional inspectors would, in effect, represent a contract between the school and the authority.

Obviously, an LEA report can confer that kind of status upon the plan. However, even where schools utilize development plans without the backing or involvement of the LEA, the idea of a contract might still be retained since:

> A plan should be operated by all teachers for it is a contract between the head and the staff to which, in the end, all must subscribe. (ILEA, 1985)

In other words, whether development plans are mandated by LEA policy or not, where they are utilized by schools then internal and external agreements should be regarded as a 'contract'. This idea is similar to Alexander's (1984) view of mutual accountability, and Elliott *et al*'s (1981) of moral accountability. It is also a practice which a number of schools already employ since some schools determine policies at staff meetings to which all staff are invited, and where staff can argue for and against proposals; but once decisions have been made (usually by the staff group, but sometimes by the head) those decisions must be adhered to. Furthermore, as new staff join the school, they too must accept those decisions until they are reviewed. This seems a sensible way of managing decisions in a professionally staffed organization. It allows for debate amongst individuals who are professionals but seeks to ensure that policy decisions are applied equally to all, so that the school as a collective (for example, as a combined teaching unit see pp. 62) sustains a sense of cohesion and consistency. Unless school development plans are regarded as contractual — either tacitly or otherwise — they run the risk of failure through staff 'opting out' of decisions they personally disagree with. Working together creates constraints and one constraint is upon individual autonomy.

Summary

Figure 6 summarizes the characteristics of school development plans. The characteristics are arranged in no significant order either clockwise or anti-clockwise. However, it is important to stress that it is the presence of all these twelve characteristics which constructs a school's development plan. The lines try to convey this since it is the interaction of the twelve lines from each of the individual characteristics which frames the plan; *the plan is the product of their interaction since it is built by their interaction.*

The relationship between having a plan and achieving success has not yet been demonstrated by research (Fullan, 1986, p.325). However, the Junior School Report (ILEA, 1986; see also Mortimore, *et al* 1988) suggests that a number of factors contribute to the effectiveness of a school. We would argue that factors 1, 2, 3, 4, 10, 11 and 12 (listed on p. 79) all feature in school development.

Figure 6: Summary of characteristics of School Development Plans

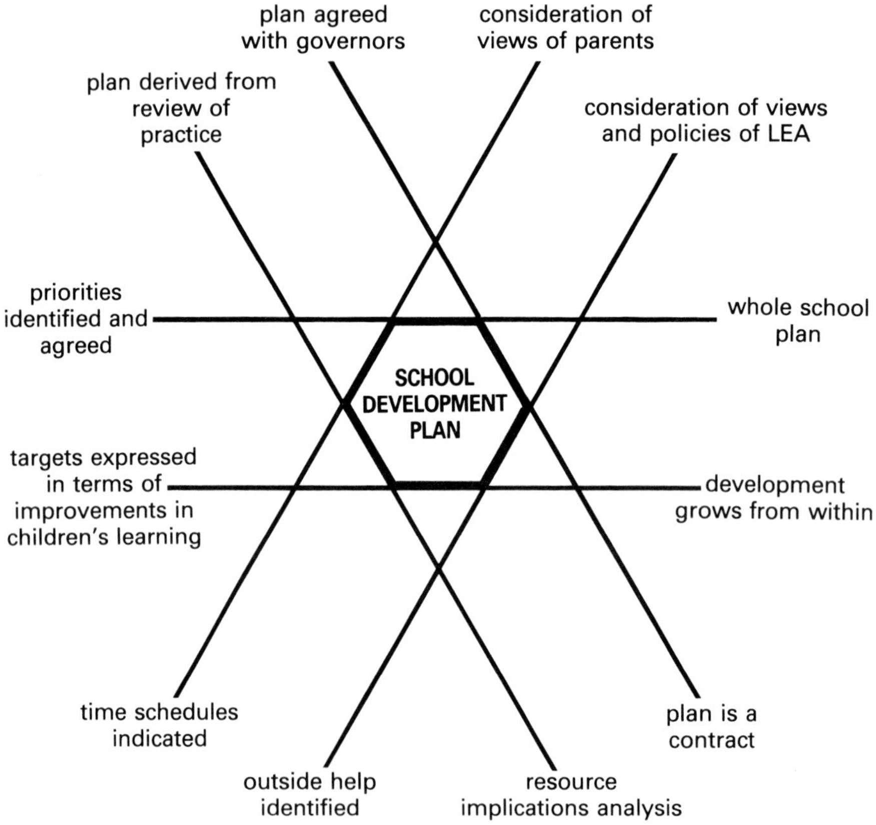

Formulating School Development Plans

The creation of a school development plan is part and parcel of a school's development culture. In stressing this point, Campbell (1987) refers to these comments by a headteacher:

> We've got to have confidence in our own leadership and our own togetherness to say, 'We're on our way and it's our journey', and I've said to the teachers . . . 'within these four walls we're largely our own salvation'.

This quotation provides some of the parameters of a school's development culture. It is a question of school-*based* development; i.e. development work which is grounded in the internal world of the school. It is growth from within. And this growth can be triggered by the formulation of a School Development Plan.

From our experience with those schools working with school development plans, we are able to make these *ten* practical suggestions:

1 The formulation of a school development plan constitutes a lengthy process; it is a case of planning — through a series of stages — over time. It is certainly not an 'over-night', once-and-for-all activity.

2 As a consequence, although a school development plan should be written down, it is very much a case of recording the staff deliberation by filing and logging the details of the planning decisions made over a period of several months.

3 Such a written record should be a 'public' document, compiled over time and circulated to all those who have had a part to play in its making or who have a need to see it. In this way it can become not only a clearly stated, public document but also one which is shared and negotiated as part of the process of its formulation.

4 In addition, the product of this process — the eventual planning document — should not be seen as 'final' and completely binding. In other words it should not be seen as a blue-print, a finally detailed strait-jacket for future action. Instead, argue Patterson *et al* (1986), it is a case of having masterful planning as opposed to a master plan. Fullan (1987) has suggested that, following the planning phase, it is very much a case of having to 'implement the implementation plan', i.e. having the space and inclination to be flexible and to be able to adapt the plan in the light of changing circumstances.

5 According to most commentators, the process of formulating a school development plan has two main components:

vision-making and path-finding
strategic planning

The process also links these two components (the generation of longer term thinking and the creation of an agenda for more immediate action) by means of a vital, intermediary stage — the identification and investigation of priority needs for development (see figure 7 below).

Figure 7:

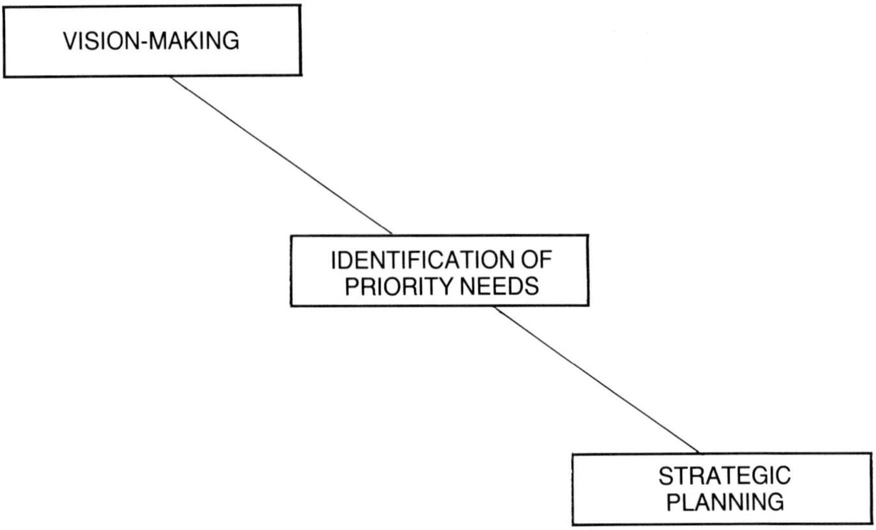

It is a bridging process which provides the practical realization, the strategic and achievable version, of the original guiding vision. Bennis and Nanus (1985) refer to this process as 'positioning' the organization by means of which areas of focus are identified for more immediate investigation.

6 What is involved here, of course, is the operation of two time perspectives, the long-term and the short-term, and, indeed, two kinds of target-setting, the general (and unfocused) and the particular (and thus more focused).

7 While the fruits of the planning process have to have meaning for individual members of staff, teams of teachers and, indeed, the staff as a whole, given the emphasis on **negotiation** and **sharing,** involvement in the planning exercise is an opportunity for enhancing staff collaboration. The process, therefore, is an ideal trigger mechanism for the staff to work collaboratively towards school-driven improvement. It is the development culture in action and embodies the principles of growth from within the school and the staff's generation and co-ownership of the development agenda. It is an opportunity, says Campbell (1987), for the staff to influence (and feel that they have influenced) the direction of the school's programme of development.

8 We have noted some confusion when commentators talk about the identification of needs. Not only is there the confusion between the various scales of involvement — is it a question of individual needs, team needs, or shared needs across the staff? — but also the confusion between **priority needs for development, in-service needs** arising from these priority needs and **process needs** such as the requirement for skill training in self-evaluation or staff collaboration. For example, a staff could identify more active approaches to learning in the classroom as *the* priority need for development and then, later in the process, realize that staff members will need workshop training in the skills of facilitating what may amount to new approaches to pupil learning. Moreover, during the process, some members of staff may identify that their need is a process one: that they would like to work together to investigate the present state of affairs in classrooms across the school and, therefore, would require training in the skills of both classroom observation and collaboration. Our stance here is that in-service needs (and, indeed, process needs) grow out of, and are determined by, the priority needs for development.

9 One of us (Holly, 1985) has argued that the process of formulating a school development plan revolves around four stages, each of which is reflected in a straightforward question:

> what do we need to look at?
> where are we now?
> where do we want to be?
> how do we get there?

These questions equate with:

> the identification of priority needs for development;
> stock-taking concerning current practice in the chosen area(s) of focus;
> shorter-term target-setting in the particular area(s) of focus;
> strategic planning in terms of a more immediate action plan (involving the identification of in-service needs) prior to implementation.

This process framework (as represented in Figure 8) indicates what should be filed in the accumulating school development plan. Such a 'log' should contain:

- details of the chosen priorities for development;
- a summary version of the evidence arising from the investigation into the nature of current practice;

- the details of the shorter-term target-setting, possibly in the form of aims and objectives;
- the details of the strategic action plan, recommendations concerning support needs (including in-service requirements) and the decisions taken.

Figure 8: Procedural (action) steps

10 Figure 8 suggests that there is a fifth question (**How are we doing?**) which represents the need over time for monitoring and evaluating the progress of the development work. Moreover, it has been argued by Patterson *et al* (1986) that the specified nature of the target-setting can be used in the form of performance indicators to check on the degree of success at the implementation stage.

> In schools, clear and shared goals provide unity, help channel and target resources within the school programme, can foster

> collaboration, **and establish criteria for school success that permit assessment of progress** . . . this takes the form of a clear vision of what the school should be, which is translated into concrete objectives and communicated to the staff in such a way as to influence what they do in their professional roles. (For both the school and the principal), written school improvement plans can be a road map for creating and realizing a shared vision of what the school should be.

Indeed, we believe that the delineation of performance indicators and their use in monitoring the development work by the teachers involved, provides a challenging, professional and developmental response.

The development processes involved in the making of a school development plan can themselves only be operationalized through the application of evaluation techniques. Indeed, Holly (1986a) has argued that these processes are essentially different approaches to evaluation and, as such, require the selection of appropriate techniques to make them happen. Some examples are as follows:

Development Processes	Appropriate Techniques	Scale of Involvement
What do we need to look at? i.e. identifying priority needs for development	GRIDS initial Survey sheet Structured staff discussion using NGT, Diamond or Snow-ball exercises	Whole staff to identify shared needs
Where are we now? i.e. reviewing current practice	Various kinds of observation Staff interviews Climate analysis	A 'research' team acting on behalf of, and reporting to, the rest of the staff
Where do we want to be? i.e. focussed target-setting	Specification of performance indicators/aims and objectives	An interest group working for the rest of the staff
How do we get there? i.e. devising an action plan	Again, a review sheet or structured discussion to identify the items for urgent attention	Another working group but directly involving colleagues in the decision-making process

Figure 9: Doing school development plans

Ten Practical Suggestions

- Treat it as a staged process over time
- Record and log the various planning decisions at different stages
- Compile a public, shared, negotiated document
- Resolve to be flexible in the implementation of the plan
- Link the major processes of vision-making and strategic planning by means of the identification of priority needs
- Incorporate both long-term and short-term considerations
- Use it as a trigger mechanism for staff collaboration and participative decision-making
- Separate priority needs for development from process needs and in-service needs
- Provide a process framework and match it with appropriate techniques
- Use performance indicators to evaluate/monitor progress

Chapter 3

Leadership in the Developing Primary School

We know that leaders make a difference to the effectiveness of an organization, be it a commercial organization or a school. For example, studies into so-called excellent commercial companies in America have described what the leaders do and how this affects the work and life of those companies (see Peters and Waterman, 1982; Peters and Austin, 1985). With reference to schools the ILEA undertook research which identified twelve key factors of effectiveness in junior schools, the first of which is 'purposeful leadership of the staff by the headteacher' (ILEA, 1986; Mortimore *et al,* 1988). Other research into school effectiveness has identified some of the features associated with successful leaders (see Reid, Hopkins and Holly, 1987). However, whilst looking at what leaders do is very important and later in this chapter we will focus on this, it is first necessary to consider what leadership is.

Leadership is difficult to define. There are numerous definitions of leadership each emphasizing some things and, often, underemphasizing others. In the absence of an agreed definition it is more useful to consider the *dimensions* of leadership since it is now recognized that leadership involves more than a single dimension (Hughes, 1985). We will briefly focus on six dimensions.

First, leaders need to *initiate structure.* That is they need to define their own role and that of others and establish clear patterns of organization, communication and methods of procedure. Second, there is *consideration* which refers to the degree to which a leader acts in a warm and supportive manner and demonstrates concern and respect for his/her colleagues. The third dimension is *decision-centralization.* This refers to the extent to which the leader influences group decisions and implies the extent to which the leader devolves decisions to others and facilitates the followers' participation in decision-making. The fourth dimension is that of the *situation* in which the leader operates since there is evidence that different situations require different things of leaders. Fifth, because of his/her position the leader is frequently, perhaps inevitably, a *model* or exemplar for the group. However, leaders can be either a positive model to be imitated or a negative model whereby followers learn behaviours to be avoided if and when they take on a leadership role. The sixth dimension is *mission*. Leadership is concerned with direction and one of the leader's tasks is to articulate and establish a sense of mission. In schools this will, in part, be the achievement of specific educational objectives, but these objectives will also point to a less precise cluster of understandings, beliefs and attitudes (Hoyle, 1986, p.112; Nias *et al,* 1989).

Of course, each of these dimensions needs further discussion, therefore if readers wish to pursue these ideas the readings cited above might make useful starting points. However, these dimensions will also be identified and highlighted in the following discussion which looks in greater detail at the nature of leadership in primary schools, at some of the implications of leading, and indicates a preferred approach for school development.

Primary School Heads As Leaders

During the 1970s and 1980s there was quite a lot of work conducted into the role and work of primary school heads. This section will attempt to present some of the ideas and findings.

Primary heads undoubtedly feel that the school is 'theirs' and that they are responsible for all that happens therein (Coulson, 1976). Consequently heads expect to determine the underlying philosophy for the school and shape the school according to their beliefs. Recent work into primary school staff relationships (Nias *et al,* 1989) confirms this outlook. Heads were shown to be either the authors, or architects (or both) of documents expressing the school's aims, curricular policies and statements to parents and governors. Moreover, both staff and heads saw it as legitimate to expect that heads' provided a sense of 'mission' for the school. Indeed, so strong was this expectation that heads provide a mission, and articulate the guiding beliefs and philosophy, that the heads were closely associated with 'their' school, and regarded as the 'owners' of the school. Staff spoke of the school as belonging to the head, whilst it is well known that heads talk about 'their' school in a special and possessive sense (Coulson, 1976; Southworth, 1987). Also, it is a feature of DES and HM Inspectors' writing that heads are depicted as being of central importance to the development of primary schools, so much so that they have been described as 'magic wands' to the school's development (see Southworth, 1986; Open University, 1988).

One outcome of this line of thinking is that leadership can become equated with headship. It is very convenient to pile up all the responsibilities and expectations onto one person. It is also both simplistic and uncomfortable. Does 'successful' head mean successful school? And does failure to develop a school mean a failing head? In truth, neither question is proper. As organizations primary schools are far too complex and intricate to allow such a crude equation of development and leadership to be tenable. Indeed, the evidence from studying effective schools suggests that whilst leadership makes a difference, so do other features and factors and leadership needs to be seen as one component amongst several others (see Mortimore *et al,* 1988) and that it is the presence of all these factors which is significant. Nevertheless, if we pull back from portraying the head as the inevitable owner of the school and from the idea that their leadership is the only reason for the school's success, then this need not necessarily relieve the head of seeking to provide a sense of mission. Rather, the sense of mission heads might need to provide is an embracing one (Hoyle, 1986, p.114), that is, one which includes staff and others and seeks to develop and sustain all the other factors of an effective school. However, a key ingredient in the notion of mission is that it should excite, stimulate and motivate *all members* of the school to try to put the mission into operation and to try to achieve it.

One obvious requirement of headteachers is that *they* can put into practice their sense of mission. This may explain why heads feel so strongly about leading through example. For this reason heads usually teach around the school, accept timetable teaching commitments, or, if they are teaching heads, use their class teaching role as a way of demonstrating their educational beliefs, philosophy and mission. It was also noted in the Primary School Staff Relationships (PSSR) project that heads used school assemblies to project and reinforce their own and their school's beliefs (Nias *et al,* 1989). Furthermore, the heads used themselves as exemplars of leadership. They encouraged and praised their colleagues. They habitually thanked the staff for their endeavours and made sure that all staff were appreciated and recognized (Southworth, 1988). In so doing the heads' behaviour embodied the leadership dimension of *consideration* and personified aspects of their mission since these heads promoted courtesy, positive reinforcement and consideration for others, as educational beliefs to foster in children. In short, the heads' behaviour was *consistent* with their beliefs. Interestingly this has also been noted in other research. Successful heads, according to Coulson (1986), have a vision of how they would like to see their schools and thus they give their schools a sense of direction but importantly they also are capable of operationalizing their goals and values both through a long-term strategy and at the level of their day-to-day actions (p.85). Similarly, Peters and Waterman (1982) noted that leaders in commerce articulated their vision and then behaved persistently, in short they mastered two ends of one spectrum: ideas at a high level of abstraction and day to day actions at the most mundane level.

Consistency means making sure that the medium is the message. Many people in leadership positions can offer a message (or mission), but what also matters is being able to work in such a way that one's actions support, sustain, nourish and reinforce that message. That might be well known but the full force of consistency actually means being able to ensure that the mundane, trivial and incidental aspects of leadership really are performed in a manner which is congruent with the message. Expressed another way, leadership is really a matter of perception: what matters to the 'followers' is how the leader *appears to behave.* What is the leader's behaviour? What does s/he do? Although for the leader, a harsh or undiplomatic word might only be a moment's irritation, for the follower, it may be their only contact with the leader that day (or week). A seemingly tiny incident to the leader may be the only piece of evidence about the leader that the 'follower' possesses for that day and it may colour — perhaps for a long time — the feelings of that individual. A real challenge for leaders is to try to behave consistently since the leaders' actions will speak louder than their words (see Peters and Austin, 1985, chapter 6).

Evidence from what heads actually do (Coulson 1976 and 1986; Nias *et al,* 1989) shows that because heads are intrigued, fascinated, even obsessed by 'their' school this helps them to be better leaders. Heads, it appears, have an unquenchable thirst for information about the school. Heads often spend a lot of time in the staffroom talking with or listening to staff. In this way they can find out how staff are feeling about both professional and personal matters and thus through their accessibility and approachability the heads further demonstrate their leadership dimension of consideration. Also, in the PSSR project the heads toured the schools observing, joining in, and seeing the school from different viewpoints. Peters and Austin (1985) call this 'MBWA' or Management By Wandering About (see also Goodchild and Holly, 1989). It is a most apt title. What takes place as part of MBWA in schools is that the head is finding out about the school. This often means that the head as leader is keeping in touch with the school as a living organization and is checking on the situational dimension. Because schools are densely populated places, and because people's feelings, health, moods, and achievements change or fluctuate it is important to be alert and sensitive to one's colleagues. Also, MBWA enables leaders to see the school from a different perspective. Moreover, it is important to consider the school's essential work — the education of children. Frequently heads are the only members of the teaching staff who have some release from class teaching duties. Therefore, through touring the school, they can see across the school and look at the curriculum in different classrooms or with different age groups. Touring the school is an informal part of school self-evaluation by the head. Heads could, of course, make it more formal if they chose to involve others. Whilst there is much to be gained by heads undertaking MBWA, is it also useful for deputies and coordinators to be given such opportunities. The extent to which a head does facilitate opportunities for other staff to observe the work taking place in other parts of the school may be an important indicator of how far decisions are decentralized.

Some Constraints On Heads As Leaders

Heads are not entirely free to do as they wish. There are various constraints and pressures upon them. The expectations of parents, governors, the LEA, staff and other colleagues can be conflicting and difficult to satisfy. Heads have to cope with multiple accountabilities and these can be constraining on the school's development either in terms of rate, scope or nature. However, these expectations and accountabilities are only one aspect of the situational factors that heads (and other leaders in the school) need to be aware of.

The nature and type of each school affects how the head and other leaders operate. For example, school size affects the head's role. A teaching head with full-time class responsibilities in a three-teacher primary school is in a very different situation to the head of a twelve-teacher school where the head does not undertake responsibility for a class group (although s/he may still teach around the school). School size affects the number of ancillary workers that are available and the number of hours they work in the school. The catchment area is another significant factor. To work in a small primary school in a rural community with supportive parents and governors is different from working in a larger, suburban school with very critical parents and governors. Indeed, one can concoct numerous such scenarios to demonstrate how the situation influences the school and therefore the head: one can also add other situational factors: the age, fabric, design and layout of the school building; the curricular strengths and weaknesses of the staff; and the 'type' of school (denominational, county, community, infant/junior/primary/first/lower). Each school's individual combination of these factors creates a distinctive context and a unique set of circumstances. Leadership is therefore contingent upon who you are leading and where (Open University, 1988, p.42) and whilst this might seem obvious such a finding is a very powerful influence upon the leader's behaviour.

Another set of constraints upon the head's leadership can be seen in the nature of the head's day-to-day existence. Because primary schools are relatively small organizations and often under-resourced (see House of Commons Select Committee, 1986) there is very little 'slack' in the organization. Ancillary workers (for example, secretaries, non-teaching assistants, meals supervisors, cleaners and caretakers) often work part-time and are therefore not always available and even when present are overloaded with an unenviable list of duties and chores. Next, almost all primary school teachers are class teachers and teach full-time with virtually no non-contact time. Frequently, the only professional with any non-contact time is the head. Therefore, when visitors call to discuss a professional matter or wish to see someone in the school it is to the head that they report. Similarly, ancillary workers may feel that there are points of procedure, housekeeping matters or pieces of information and messages that a professional needs to know about, thus they too inform the head about these matters simply because everyone else is teaching. Furthermore, because in medium and larger primary schools the head is notionally relieved of class teaching responsibilities, when teaching staff are absent through ill-health it is common for the head to be expected and required by the LEA to cover for absent colleagues — at least for the first few days. This sometimes reduces the head's role to that of a supply teacher (Southworth, 1985a) and means that they have to jettison or postpone planned developments in the school.

When heads keep diaries of their working days or conduct analyses of their use of time (Manasse, 1985; Clerkin 1985; Coulson 1986; Craig, 1987) a number of features can be identified:

- Heads appear to spend much of their time working at a high intensity of tasks, many of which are unrelated and some of which are non-essential.
- There is a danger that sometimes heads become over-involved with minor tasks or with tasks which lie within someone else's province but who, because they are part-time workers, are not available during parts of the day to attend to matters (for example, caretakers and building repairs).

- Heads spend much of their time in face-to-face communication with staff, pupils and visitors.
- The primary school head's role is essentially about dealing with people and they need to be accessible and approachable.
- Planned work often suffers because of unplanned events and incidents.

All of these points are made by Clerkin (1985) who goes on to say:

> Headteacher activity is more often about tackling a high intensity of tasks with frequent interruptions rather than a systematic ordering of curricular or organizational programmes based on agreed policies or clearly understood management structures . . . energy is devoted to 'keeping the school ticking over' in the short term with only limited opportunity to consider important longer term issues.
>
> Since the effective leader is most likely to be a person who successfully manages to combine long-term considerations with more immediate tasks there is good reason . . . to encourage the head to involve other staff more fully in school business.

A Way Forward

Putting the above two sections together indicates the following picture. Heads play an important role in providing a sense of mission. Their mission offers some direction for their schools and usually provides a sense of purpose and a way forward. However, heads do not have a free hand in providing this mission, they need to be sensitive to the expectations of colleagues and partners (governors, parents, children, staff, LEA, community). This sensitivity is often visible in how considerate they are towards colleagues and others. Moreover, because consideration is often a key element in both their mission and its implementation, heads simultaneously believe in consideration as a worthwhile attribute and as an instrumental and necessary tactic which helps them influence the staff as a collective group. Having articulated their mission, heads need to secure their staffs' commitment to it. Consideration plays a part here, since being considerate to colleagues is part of the individual negotiation (and manipulation) which takes place between staff (see Nias *et al,* 1989). Thus heads may be considerate both for reasons of principle and pragmatism. Heads also use influence at times of staff selection, internal organization and when initiating structures (allocation of classes, timetables, responsibilities, leadership roles etc.). Lastly, heads seek to influence through their own example.

However, much of the heads' exemplary behaviour may be absorbed by coping with mundane, trivial, non-essential tasks and incidents, or in responding to unplanned and unexpected events. Whilst they need to demonstrate that their involvement with such tasks will not deter or deflect them from the pursuit of the school's mission, the cumulative effect of day-to-day incidents, with their characteristic fragmentation of attention and effort, may be to decelerate the pace of school development. For some heads this pattern of work can mean that all their energies go into maintaining the school rather than contributing to or facilitating its development. Therefore, unless others in the school can continue the developmental work the school may not move forward. The participation of others is thus vital to the notion of development.

This outline of the head as leader shows that the head's work involves all the discussed dimensions of leadership: mission, consideration, initiation of structure, modelling, situational awareness and decision-decentralization. Yet the head's work also shows that there are two powerful sets of reasons for heads decentralizing decision-making and involving others in the leadership of the school. First, participation and collaboration are needed because a school is a *collective.* Whilst leaders might be expected to provide a mission and direction for the school that mission, in most cases, has to be both appropriate to the school's situation and considerate of the staff's circumstances. Mission has to be contingent upon who it is for. Without most or all members of a school being involved with, and committed to, the prevailing mission (to which hopefully they have also contributed) then in reality there is no effective mission for the school. Second, collaboration is needed because the head can neither singlehandedly impose his/her mission nor does s/he always have sufficient time and resources to be free of other tasks. Heads are often vulnerable to the vagaries of day-to-day life in school. The unplanned, unexpected and urgent can often overtake their intentions and day-to-day plans. Therefore, it is not surprising that during the 1980s there has been a demand for collaborative work (Alexander, 1984; Campbell, 1985; Thomas, 1987) and shared leadership (Southworth, 1985b, 1986 and 1987; Open University, 1988).

Deputy Heads And Shared Leadership

Another of the key factors of school effectiveness identified by the ILEA research team (Mortimore *et al,* 1988; ILEA, 1986) was the involvement of the deputy head:

> The Junior School Project findings indicate that the deputy head can have a major role in the effectiveness of junior schools. Where the deputy was frequently absent, or absent for a prolonged period (due to illness, attendance on long courses, or other commitments), this was detrimental to pupils' progress and development. Moreover, a change of deputy tended to have negative effects.
>
> The responsibilities undertaken by deputy heads also seemed to be important. Where the head generally involved the deputy in policy decisions, it was beneficial to the pupils. This was particularly true in terms of allocating teachers to classes. Thus, it appeared that a certain amount of delegation by the headteacher, and a sharing of responsibilities, promoted effectiveness. (ILEA, 1986, p.35)

Of course such a finding merely confirms what experience and commonsense has always told heads, deputies and teachers. When the head and deputy work productively together they reduce discontinuities between themselves as school leaders. Such working together is usually called a partnership and whilst the claimed benefits of partnership are considerable and frequent (see Waters, 1987; Open University, 1988) there is a need to discern what such partnerships might mean and look like in practice.

The first characteristic of a head and deputy's partnership is specificity. Since the head's role is, in part, contingent upon the particular circumstances of the school's situation, so too will the deputy's role be influenced by the school's context and circumstances (Open University 1988). However, the deputy's role is also contingent upon the individual head — his/her mission, educational philosophy, management skills, curricular priorities and personal predilections. In turn, the head will be influenced by the deputy's philosophies, strengths and personal qualities. Therefore, the nature of their relationship and partnership will be a specific blend of all these factors. Importantly, the two will 'negotiate' areas of match and mismatch in their individual perspectives and roles. The extent and nature of their match/mismatch will affect where and how the two complement and supplement each other, or more negatively where they may disagree and even conflict with each other. As Whitaker says, an:

> . . . interesting consideration arises out of the comparative philosophies, personalities, and management styles of the head

> and deputy. Some heads are very conscious of this and deliberately set out to recruit a deputy who will complement their own qualities and thus bring a wide range of attitudes and ideas into the school. More perhaps go for the closest possible match to their own philosophy and personality in the belief that a doubling of the driving forces will help to bring about the changes they wish to see. (Whitaker, 1983, p.87)

Other characteristics of this partnership can be seen in Nias' useful case study of an infant school headteacher and deputy (Nias, 1987). Nias notes, in common with other research, that the deputy's role lacked definition. It was largely based upon negotiated ways of working with the head rather than on defined and prescribed tasks. However, it was clear that the deputy accepted a subordinate position and that it was the head who was the senior partner. Thus, the partnership was characterized not by symmetry but by an acceptance by both parties of its asymmetry. Yet detailed examination of what the head and deputy *actually did* nevertheless showed the deputy to be a person of considerable influence in the school. Though not defined the deputy's role complemented the head's. She played a central role in the school's formal and informal communication systems, undertook administrative tasks and kept staff morale high. Moreover, the deputy also acted as a confidante to the head who in turn, used her as a sounding board in the formulation and prosecution of the school's goals. What emerges from the study is that the deputy's *informal* activity was as important as her formal activity.

The fact that the head and deputy complemented each other is an important characteristic. While they adopted through negotiation, accommodation and habit some roles which were differentiated, the head and deputy were also similar:

> So, for example, both the head and the deputy had a communication function, both undertook administration, both took assembly, both were alert to staff's personal and professional problems. Moreover, each could, and often did, temporarily take over the other's role. Small though the school was, as a system, it contained elements of what Landau (1969) has described as redundancy. Like a commercial airliner, its structure enabled every vital function to be carried out by more than one component, creating in its members (and its users) confidence in its security and strength.
>
> The overlapping, duplication and substitution which resulted made the school's leadership relatively impervious to shock, absence, and disruption of routine. The fact that head and

> deputy could be nourished (one might say refuelled) not only within the organization but by each other, increased their confidence in the efficiency and effectiveness of the school. Their resulting sense of security and stability encouraged all the staff to be more relaxed and protected them all against an expenditure of nervous energy on unproductive ends. In other words, the head and deputy had evolved a system which gave them a degree of 'slack', a term used by management theoriest (for example, Cyert and March, 1963) to describe spare resources which can be used to cushion an organization against uncertainty. At a time when many primary schools face considerable uncertainty, induced, for example, by financial cuts, falling rolls, amalgamations, redeployment, accountability pressures, curriculum debate, the deputy may, by effectively doubling the school's leadership potential, play a crucial role in helping a school to adapt productively to a changing environment. (Nias, 1987, p.51)

In other words, the head and deputy's partnership contributed to the school's organizational health and resilience. This is a compelling case for heads and deputies to work together as partners but there are certain riders to add. First, in advocating a head/deputy partnership one is not suggesting an exclusive partnership. The head and deputy need to be able to act as partners but not at the expense of the staff. Their partnership should enable all other staff to feel involved in the school's work and mission, and to participate in its realization. The partnership should not be injurious to teachers' perceptions and feelings about the nature of their own participation in the school and with the head and deputy as individuals.

Second, much of Nias' case study demonstrates that this partnership benefits the school's *organizational* development. Yet, as chapter 1 says, primary school development needs to occur on a broad front of interrelated and interpenetrating developments (for example, organizational, curricular, teacher, child). Therefore, we need to consider how the deputy and head's organizational partnership can contribute, say, to formal curricular development. In short, whilst the picture Nias presents of a partnership is illuminating it may not be sufficient. Therefore, the position adopted by the ILEA's Committee on Primary Education Report (1985) offers further guidance:

> . . . we consider it necessary that all deputy heads should be required to lead sections of the staff and occasionally the whole staff in the formulation of school policies including curricular policies . . . they should also in the course of time, have

> experience of the various tasks for which heads are responsible including taking part in interviews for staff and preparing the various returns that have to be made to the authority. If they are not members in their own right, they should be allowed, occasionally, to attend governors' meetings as observers.

This outlook means that the deputy is simultaneously being prepared for any future promotion and, for these occasions when they are required to deputize for the head. Moreover, there is also a clear requirement that the deputy performs a formal leadership role in curriculum policy making and decision-taking.

Waters (1987) has provided a description of what a deputy's formal responsibilities should include. They cover such things as: administration (forms, communications, pupil transfers and records, emergency procedures); ritual practices (assemblies, ceremonies, welcome of planned visitors, intake meetings for pupils' parents); governors; classroom development; curriculum responsibility and leadership; managing meetings; parent organizations; deputizing. A deputy head needs to be involved across all of these areas. This helps him/her develop a 'whole' school perspective, enables them to supplement the head's and staff's perceptions, and means that the deputy is seen to be involved across the school by both 'insiders' (staff and children) and 'outsiders' (governors, parents, LEA officials). Not only should a deputy do these things but s/he should be seen to be doing all of these things by all of these people since this will help to confer status upon the deputy.

A number of reasons have now been presented which begin to show how a partnership can benefit head, deputy, staff and school. Clearly the partnership needs to be sensitively negotiated, agreed, monitored and adapted in the light of the school's changing circumstances. In essence the argument rests on a belief that two heads are better than one. Since, at present, headteachers are doubly burdened with expectations to develop the school and cope with all kinds of essential and non-essential administrative chores and tasks it is both expedient to delegate some of their work, and consistent with beliefs in collaboration to involve the deputy in policy-making and school leadership. Moreover, beliefs in collaboration will be better served when the head and deputy can act as a model of collaboration for other staff to emulate. The head-deputy partnership is thus *symbolic:* if the head and deputy cannot collaborate what chance is there for anyone else in the school?

Leadership For Participation

Several reasons for heads involving staff have now been noted. However, there are some others which should be added.

The PSSR project identified, from an analysis of the case studies of five primary schools, two important features of primary school leadership (Nias *et al,* 1989). First, the heads' leadership was enhanced because they could occupy two roles — leader and *member.* On many occasions the heads of the project schools were members of the staff group. That is, they did not isolate themselves from the staff group; they were not aloof nor distant. Most of the time they were to be found in the staffroom, listening, talking, and laughing with staff colleagues. Moreover, they were willing to take a 'back seat' when someone else was leading a meeting or a discussion. Membership meant that the heads were sometimes first among equals, or sometimes just equal. Second, a central finding was that each school had either installed or was installing a 'culture of collaboration'. This culture was, in effect, the existence among the staff group of commonly held, though often unspoken, beliefs and values which affected how the staff group behaved. These beliefs were: acceptance of the individual, acceptance of interdependence and belief in the value of interpersonal openness. Thus, teachers and ancillaries both *believed in* collaboration and *behaved* collaboratively. It also appears that this 'collaborative culture' was created and that it was an aspect of each head's mission that collaboration was seen as important and necessary to the school's development.

It may well be that such a culture or something similar exists in the schools which the ILEA junior project reported on since another of the school effectiveness factors is the involvement of teachers:

> In successful schools, the teachers were involved in curriculum planning and played a major role in developing their own curriculum guidelines. As with the deputy head, teacher involvement in decisions concerning which classes they were to teach, was important. Similarly, consultation with teachers about decisions on spending, was important. It appeared that schools in which teachers were consulted on issues affecting school policy, as well as those affecting them directly, were more likely to be successful. (ILEA, 1986)

These two sets of findings (PSSR and ILEA) add weight to the calls for staff to work collaboratively (see Southworth, 1987; Thomas, 1987). Further, the findings of HM Inspectors support this viewpoint and describe what such collaboration looks like. In their document *Primary*

Schools: Some Aspects of Good Practice, HM Inspectors provide an overview of the characteristics of good practice in the schools:

> In each school the head and staff had agreed aims relating to the academic work and the children's personal and social development. A shared sense of purpose was most evident in the way teachers talked to their pupils . . . Most of the schools had curricular guidelines which had been carefully thought out. In almost all cases these guidelines had been written after staff discussions at meetings led by one teacher or a small group of teachers able to offer informed advice on the particular aspect of the curriculum . . . A certain proportion of the schemes at work were being reviewed at the time of inspections . . . A number of the schools were exploring ways of deploying the staff so that more effective use was made of their abilities and curricular strengths . . . the schools were making positive efforts to strike the delicate balance which is involved in making the best use of the curricular expertise of a primary school staff as a combined teaching unit. (DES, 1987)

Earlier reference was made to the school being a collective, whilst the discussion on shared leadership and participation has focussed on the need for teachers to be involved in decision-making. However, HM Inspectors introduce the notion of a school's staff acting as a 'combined teaching unit'. This is a significant extension of the discussion. Collaboration, rather like the head and deputy's partnership, is not simply a good idea because it helps the school-as-an-organization function more smoothly, it is worthwhile because it is a process which enables the interests, skills and expertise of each teacher (indeed, member of staff) to spread across the staff group. Expressed another way, collaboration is not just a way for staff to 'rub along together' it is also the way that skills 'rub off' on each other. The heart of the matter is that leadership and participation should be orchestrated so that staff work together in order that their teaching is combined in ways that are mutually supportive. If that can be achieved the staff's work becomes more than the sum of its parts.

Such arguments can of course sound rather idealistic since participation and collaboration sound wonderfully 'democratic'; but primary schools are not always (if ever) democratic places. The responsibilities of headteachers tend to inhibit such a stance. Moreover, another difficulty with participative decision-making is that it is all too easily taken to mean decision-making by consensus. Consensus is usually good when it occurs but some decisions concerning developments and change might never happen if we wait for consensus. Instead, leaders might be better advised to settle for *consent.* Consent means only that the majority of a group agree to give an idea a try, whereas consensus usually means everyone being fully sold on the idea. Consent is thus more realistic and less idealistic.

Another problem is that of actually developing a combined teaching unit. Clearly this is rather more than simply getting people together and holding a few staff meetings. A lot of work needs to be done to bring people together. This means that the social climate has to be healthy rather than hostile (see Nias *et al,* 1989) hence the 'affective relationships' need to be considered so that those in leadership positions can respond and support others (See Day, Johnson, Whitaker, 1985, pp.112-9). Yet whilst this sounds daunting progress can be made by thinking about the obvious and the ordinary. It is important that the staffroom be a pleasant place for staff to congregate. Decent chairs and facilities can make a big difference. Other resources like copiers, printers and some access to the school secretary and typewriting can make staff feel that their curricular documents, working papers and discussion documents are valued and it also eases their workload by relieving some of the pressure in producing documents. Release from class teaching to visit colleagues' classrooms during the working day can support a great deal of work, whilst small blocks of released time 'buy' a lot of goodwill. Recognition of each other's efforts also generates positive feelings and this all drip-feeds development. Developing a climate for development need not always involve spectacular changes. Rather, development is often about lots of seemingly ordinary things attended to with a persistence and a sensitivity which makes the sum of them extraordinary.

Conclusion

Throughout this discussion of leadership and participation there have been generalized descriptions and illustrations from practice. There are two reasons for this. First, many schools are already working along these lines. Second, what is being promoted must be *doable.* If schools are to develop they need to be offered realistic models; they need to try things which they can do. At various points we have noted that actions speak louder than words: That there needs to be consistency between the leader's rhetoric and his/her behaviour. Similarly, if a developing school needs lots of leaders then all of these leaders need to be doing things which are productive. But whatever each of them does needs to be within their capabilities; it is about tasks that people can do, tasks that turn the average performer into a star or enables the average performer to find that there is a star within her/his self (Peters and Austin, 1985).

All of this builds into a formidable challenge: lots of leaders, enabling leadership, partnership, participation, MBWA, the school as a combined teaching unit. It is more than any one person can realistically hope to manage, particularly when that person is called 'headteacher' and they have to simultaneously concentrate on so many other things: from LMS to special needs, vandalism to non-accidental injury, Aids to early years education, science and technology to leaking toilets. Furthermore, no one person can manage all this. What they can do, however, is orchestrate it (Southworth, 1987). If the head is orchestrator of all the other leaders and members then maybe the school will work and play in greater harmony. Orchestration was introduced in chapter one, suffice it to say here that leadership is also about the orchestration of at least six dimensions of leadership (structure, consideration, decision-decentralization, situation, modelling and mission) to facilitate the development of other leaders, members of staff, the children and hence the school.

Chapter 4

Managing School Development in the Primary School

The case for schools requiring lots of leaders was made in the previous chapter. Although the power of the headteacher has not diminished, and legislation during the 1980s has constantly emphasized the headteacher's responsibilities, the task of school development is fundamentally a shared task. Furthermore, because the head is often called upon to deal with unexpected unplanned and varied issues his/her leadership is vulnerable to competing demands. The role of the deputy head was therefore considered since a partnership between head and deputy should reduce discontinuities in leadership if the head and deputy can substitute for each other. However, whilst heads can spend significant amounts of time engaged on a variety of 'maintenance' tasks which ensure that the school, on a day to day basis, works reasonably smoothly, the head is often protecting staff from any number of interruptions to and distractions from their teaching. The head is therefore *enabling* staff to proceed with the main purpose of the school, the education of the children. In which case one might ask who is leading, the head or staff? When the head is busy in dealing with parental concerns, building repairs, administration, case conferences, or lost coats (see Court, 1987) it is very likely that others are leading. Moreover, because a school is a collective, comprised of teachers, ancillaries, children, and voluntary helpers and because schools are organized on the basis of one teacher to a group or class of children, *curriculum leadership* is effectively devolved to each teacher.

One of the things which distinguishes primary school teaching from secondary teaching is that there is just one teacher for all or most of the child's schooling for a period of one year and often longer (Alexander, 1984, p.13). This means that:

> the class teacher gets to know the children well and provides a sense of security and continuity;

> the teacher is responsible for trying to ensure that the whole curriculum for that group of children fits together or 'coheres';
>
> the teacher can arrange the work to cater for individual children's demands and needs;
>
> the teacher can take advantage of planned and unplanned opportunities without disrupting colleagues' programmes of work (adapted from ILEA, 1985).

In turn, this means that class teachers must attempt to do two things. First, they must try to teach the 'whole child', that is to try 'to understand the many facets of the child's development, his/her interests, aspirations, abilities and potential — verbal, expressive, physical and so on' (Alexander, 1984, p.13). Second, the class teacher is obliged to plan, implement, review and evaluate the 'whole curriculum' for each child. Therefore, class teaching brings some disadvantages:

> it is almost inevitable, since no teacher is equally good at all areas of the curriculum, that some areas are covered better than others; demands for new skills in teaching and developments in certain curriculum areas (for example, technology, designing and making) mean that the teacher's role in planning and evaluation is increasing (adapted from ILEA, 1985; see also Open University, 1988, p.36).

Therefore, the class teaching system in primary schools means that primary teachers are curriculum leaders for their class and that there are advantages and disadvantages to this. HM Inspectors, in their Primary Survey (DES, 1978b) were keenly aware of both points when they said:

> The critical points are: can class teachers manage to provide all that is necessary for particular classes? If not, what must be done to help them to manage satisfactorily and in a way that is, on balance, advantageous? (para 8.44)

By way of an answer to these questions HM Inspectors, in the 1978 Primary Survey, and elsewhere emphasized the role of the curriculum postholder:

> 8.45 It is disappointing to find that the great majority of teachers with posts of special responsibility have little influence at present on the work of other teachers. Consideration needs to be given to improving their standing, which is the product of the ways in which the teachers with special posts regard themselves and also of the attitudes that other teachers have towards them.

> 8.46 It is important that teachers with special responsibility for, say, mathematics should, in consultation with the head, other members of staff and teachers in neighbouring schools, draw up the scheme of work to be implemented in the school; give guidance and support to other members of staff; assist in teaching mathematics to other classes when necessary; and be responsible for the procurement, within the funds made available, of the necessary resources for teaching the subject. They should develop acceptable means of assessing the effectiveness of the guidance and resources they provide, and this may involve visiting other classes in the school to see the work in progress. (DES, 1978b)

The naming of these teachers has proved something of a problem since they were variously known as teachers in posts of special responsibility, scale postholders, curriculum leaders, consultants, advisers or co-ordinators. Whilst acknowledging that they fulfil a leadership role we shall hitherto refer to them as curriculum coordinators (although cited sources may refer otherwise to them). The 1978 Primary Survey added greatly to the significance and status of curriculum coordinators. HM Inspectors summarized the role as:

> 8.64 Teachers in posts of special responsibility need to keep up-to-date in their knowledge of their subject; to be familiar with its main concepts, with the sub-divisions of the subject material and how they relate to one another. They have to know enough of available teaching materials and teaching approaches to make and advise upon choices that suit local circumstances. And they should be aware of the ways in which children learn and of any sequences of learning that need to be taken into account. Additionally, these teachers should learn how to lead groups of teachers and to help others to teach material which is appropriate to the abilities of the children. They should learn how to establish a programme of work in cooperation with other members of staff and how to judge whether it is being operated successfully. They should also learn how to make the best use of the strengths of teachers of all ages and to help them to develop so that they may take on more responsibility. Particular care should be taken to foster the special qualities of intuitive and gifted teachers. Heads need, in consultation with those concerned, to make quite clear the responsibilities of individual teachers. (*ibid*, pp.124-5).

This role description expanded and elaborated the coordinator's role (Campbell, 1985) and when this role was reinforced by, for example, the National Union of Teachers (NUT 1979), and the Cockcroft Report (DES, 1982), it became clear that coordination was *the* major way in which HM Inspectors, the DES, and others, were attempting to improve quality in curriculum provision in primary schools. It is therefore worthwhile looking at what we have learned from the work of coordinators since they have been central to recent strategies and processes in the management of curriculum and school development.

What Have We Learned?

Thirteen points will be noted about what we have learned about curriculum coordination.

First, the work of curriculum coordinators implicitly assumes that school-based curriculum development is 'a good thing'. In its own way so too does this book. Yet, whilst we agree with the value assumptions of school-based development, it is clear from what we now know about curriculum coordinators (see, for example, Taylor, 1986; Primary School Research and Development Group/Schools Council, 1983; Goodacre, 1984) that school-based development is complex, involving three main features. First, that teachers be collaborative. Second that teachers draw upon the specialist expertise of each other. Third, that internal relationships in respect of authority, classroom autonomy and curriculum activity are critical to any notion of development (Campbell, 1985).

Second, job descriptions have become common in primary schools, and part of their proliferation is as a consequence of defining the role of coordinators. Although job descriptions are a sensible way of allocating responsibilities and providing some clarity to the organization of the school there is a tendency for job descriptions to be overly detailed. Some descriptions were actually specifications and ran to over eighteen itemized tasks! However, it was often the case that curriculum coordinators had clearer job descriptions than deputies, and that the job descriptions embodied some implicit messages about authority inside the primary school. Coordinators were usually seen as directly responsible to the headteacher. Rarely were they responsible to the deputy head, head of department (if there was one) or to the staff group as a whole. Consequently, it was all too easy for the coordinator to be perceived merely as the agent of the head's desired changes and for them to be working on behalf of the head, rather than the school as a whole. Whilst the coordinator was likely to be working in ways congruent with the head's wishes, preferences and 'mission', they may have created a sense of disharmony if the head had not secured everyone else's commitment to the changes. Therefore, job descriptions may have provided some clarity concerning the allocation of tasks to individuals, but they also carried important messages about authority and harmony in the school.

Third, the authority of the coordinator often rested upon their personal qualities and standing with colleagues. Unless the coordinator was perceived to be 'a good teacher', able to 'get on' with others and to offer both effective advice/support (for example, 'That's a good idea') and with efficiency (for example, 'doesn't waste time in meetings' or 'always orders resources in time') then the coordinator's role was adversely affected, if not crippled. Example is a powerful belief in primary schools (see Nias *et al,* 1989) and coordinators needed (still need) to lead through example. Furthermore, authority through example extended to two other features of life in primary schools. One of these features concerns 'through-school expertise'. Primary teachers not only need to demonstrate some competence, or expertise, in their designated curriculum area (for example, to be a 'good' teacher of art or maths or music) but also need to be able to teach children of all ages in the school. In a primary school with children aged from four to eleven, therefore, if a teacher was perceived not to be experienced or capable with, say, young children (for example, 'he knows little about infants') then the teachers of those young children might have exempted themselves from the coordinator's influence and authority. The other feature to report concerns the expansion of curriculum areas which were seen as being in need of development. Science, designing and making (or CDT as it was initially called), and computers were all emphasized during the early and mid-1980s. In some schools teachers needed only to have a slight inclination towards one (or more) of those areas before becoming the designated coordinator! Whilst it looked good to 'outsiders' that the school had a coordinator for the latest emphasis, to the 'insiders', and the individual coordinator, the degree of 'expertise' was sometimes rather slight. The contribution that such individuals could make to curriculum development was consequently limited because the coordinator's authority and confidence as an expert was sometimes too shallow.

Fourth, (Campbell, 1985) has shown that time was a major problem because there was a general lack of it. There was little time available for coordinators to work with teachers during the school day. There was also little opportunity for coordinators to consider 'through-school' matters (for example, work going on with different age groups). Therefore, a teacher of older children could not easily gain insight into the teaching and learning of young children. Moreover, much of the coordinator's work in terms of supporting colleagues took place in 'snatched times': informal conversations, ad hoc 'meetings' in twos and threes, and classroom 'visits' during lunch breaks, playtimes, or 'manufactured moments' (for example, assemblies, story-times). These constituted much, perhaps in some case the majority, of occasions for influencing others. Working groups and meetings, usually after school, represented the principal formal occasions for sharing ideas, plans, making decisions and reviewing practice. Yet before 1987 when 'direct time' was introduced, such meetings were seen as 'voluntary' and competed with other activities (for example, clubs, sports). Lastly, it was obvious that coordinators invested large amounts of their personal time to the production of documents, working papers, requisitions and schemes of work since these were commonly done at home.

Fifth, curriculum coordinators were somewhat ambivalent about their role. They did not always feel they could direct colleagues or enforce their ideas. Generally, they tended to write documents (schemes of work, guidelines, subject aims), order resources for others, offer 'tips' (survival strategies?) or provide advice (ideas, management of resources). Much of their work was *consultative,* and might be described as the 'soft' part of the role. Undoubtedly, they felt ambivalent about their authority and often thought that only the head could, or should, be directive or the 'strong' leader. Also, there was evidence that coordinators lacked confidence and needed help in being assertive (Goodacre, 1984). Yet, whatever the reasons, coordinators did not in our experience appear to regularly comment on colleagues' teaching styles, approach, lesson content or plans. Coordinators did not appear to act (with any regularity) as critical friends to colleagues, at least judging by HM Inspectors' reports, published reports on school inspections, feedback from INSET courses in East Anglia, or the literature. Whether they should have is, of course, an interesting question, but the fact that they did not, even though their school might simultaneously be undertaking self-evaluation, is noteworthy. It suggests a possible reluctance to be critical, or overtly judgmental. It might also imply that consideration, tact, respect for individuality, and autonomy meant more to primary teachers and constrained frank and open discussion of differences than HM Inspectors had recognized when they advocated a role for coordinators.

Sixth, implicit to the job of the coordinator was the idea that they would influence and change practice (see DES, 1978b, para 8.45 cited above), yet coordinators were never properly equipped for this role. Opportunities were limited to attend INSET courses concerned with understanding the processes of *change*. Those coordinators who did study change often did so on a DIY basis (through In-service BEd, Advanced

Diplomas, MEd, and MA programmes) rather than on behalf of the school or as part of LEAs support for coordinators. The extent to which LEAs mounted local courses on innovation, implementation, curriculum planning, evaluation, and school development for primary teachers was not large, particularly in relation to courses dealing with curriculum content (for example, mathematics, science, special needs, language, reading) which were more widespread. Further, as Campbell (1985) showed, the coordinators' job entailed working with colleagues, and the opportunities for coordinators to develop interpersonal skills were also restricted. In truth, coordinators were not well prepared for the job expected of them.

If the sixth point is critical of external preparation and support for coordination then the seventh point arises from the lack of 'internal' support. Headteachers did not consistently help coordinators to do their job. The extent to which heads enabled coordinators to function no doubt varied considerably, but the impression given by many coordinators was that their heads (for whatever reasons) were not doing enough to help them. Coordinators *felt* they needed either more time, money, personal development, or authority — in some cases they felt they needed more of all of them!

The eighth thing we have learned is that the curriculum focus was largely subject-based. This might have under-emphasized cross-curricular issues (for example, equal opportunities). In a sense, coordinators were expected to coordinate aspects of the school's work because class teaching created 'fragmentation' in the school. With primary schools being organized into a series of class groups, each under the charge of a single teacher, the structure of primary schools fosters independence rather than interdependence (Coulson, 1976). This gave rise to calls for curriculum continuity (Dean, 1980; Benyon, 1982) since it appeared to some that, whilst class teachers provided coherence for the children during the time in which that individual teacher was responsible for them, coherence did not necessarily occur amongst teachers as children moved from class to class, and teacher to teacher, over a period of several years. One expectation of coordinators was that they would coordinate, in respect of their curriculum area, across the school to reduce discontinuities and inconsistencies. However:

> The creation of coordinators working across the school may, at one and the same time, be a response to the fragmentation caused by independent class teachers and a cause of another kind of fragmentation with the 'whole curriculum' divided into curriculum areas. It is, perhaps, only the substitution of one kind of fragmentation for another. (Open University, 1988)

Absent in the literature on coordinators was any attention to who should coordinate the coordinators. It was probable that this was seen as a task for heads (or perhaps deputies) but the lack of appreciation for this task, and how it might be attempted, suggests that it was either unrecognized or underestimated. Certainly, if no-one was consciously fitting the work of coordinators together it is difficult to understand how schools could have been developing 'whole school' approaches.

In addition to these eight points we should add five more from Campbell (1985). It is useful to look at Campbell's views because he asked the question what did coordinators achieve? He is convinced that changes did occur but 'the central issue is whether these changes were improvements and, if so, in what sense' (*ibid,* p.60). Campbell believes that because coordinators (postholders he called them) were breaking new ground it was only realistic to talk about what they were beginning to achieve, to look at what new processes were emerging and to think about what approaches were being established. Using his own case studies Campbell noted five areas where new developments emerged:

1 **Continuity and consistency in a subject through the school**

Moves were made to establish consistency and coherence in the schools' curricula by the provision of explicit statements of concepts and skills to be covered in particular areas. Also, reviews of existing practices, revisions to existing schemes, adoption and implementation and evaluation of revisions to schemes did take place.

2 **Enhanced staff confidence in the subject and respect for the postholder's expertise**

Confidence, albeit slowly, was raised. In small and apparently routine ways, teachers' confidence was built up by the coordinators. 'There was nothing dramatic about the change in confidence levels — indeed the way it was done was almost incidental to other, more apparently mainstream, purposes but it was present in all cases' (p.62).

3 **Collective decision-making**

Given the opportunity to participate in decision-making, most teachers in Campbell's researched schools took it 'intelligently and responsibly', yet it was also precise to say that school decision-making was by the active participants in working groups, 'rather than by the whole collectivity of the staff, some of whom did not participate at all . . . or passively accepted what was proposed' when the whole staff met together in staff meetings (p.63).

4 **Devolution of responsibility**

The heads reported that they had planned for collective decision-making to occur by encouraging groups of staff to work together, and this did more or less happen.

5 The coordinator as educationist
Coordinators deployed their subject expertise, wrote up staff's objectives for revisions to schemes of work and had to provide elaborate justification for the approaches taken. In so doing coordinators apprehended aspects of educational research and theory and had to 'translate' this for colleagues. In all of this the teachers were extending their role from teacher to educationalist. Coordinators 'enabled new schemes of work to be created, revised policies to be implemented and innovations to be evaluated, but that they had done so by exercising a role in which the principles upon which change had been predicted were made explicit to their professional peers . . . the extension of their role in this way led to the development of their own professional abilities as well as of the curriculum itself' (based on Campbell, 1985, pp.60-5).

When Campbell's five points are added to the previous eight, it can be seen that, since 1978, we have learned much about coordination in terms of emerging benefits, constraints to be overcome and issues to resolve. Yet, even as these points were becoming obvious others continued to promote the role.

Further Support For Coordinators

The House of Commons Select Committee's report on *Achievement in Primary Schools* (1986) gave a further boost to the role of coordinators. To begin with the Select Committee agreed that, on balance, it is advantageous to maintain the class teacher system as far as possible but 'it is unreasonable to expect one teacher to cope with the depth and width of the modern primary curriculum' (para. 9.9). The Committee noted that there are two ways of proceeding when a class teacher is in difficulty with regard to a part of the curriculum: 'One is to provide the teacher with the advice and support that will enable him or her to proceed. The other is to arrange for someone else to take over the teaching' (para 9.10). The Committee, whilst accepting a place for the second, preferred the first. They then looked at who might be coordinators and what should they do.

With reference to who should be a coordinator the Committee said: 'it should be part of the ordinary duties of virtually every primary school teacher to act as a coordinator in some aspect of primary school work' (para 9.17). Interestingly, the Committee speaks of 'work' rather than 'curriculum' which means, presumably, that coordinators need not necessarily be confined to curriculum areas or subjects but could be responsible for aspects of the school as an organization (for example, early years, teams of teachers, year groups). With reference to the role of coordinators the Committee said:

What should coordinators do?

9.19 Many of our witnesses thought the two principal functions of coordinators were to advise other teachers and, occasionally to work with children alongside their class teacher. We were strongly warned against specialist teaching on a secondary school model mainly on the grounds that to introduce it would disadvantageously fragment the children's work and reduce the quality of personal relationships, but also because the introduction would be organizationally difficult in small schools. Others warned that any change of practice should be limited to the older children or to certain subjects. Some wanted any changes carefully monitored, taking into account the effects on parents as well as on schools.

9.20 We accept unreservedly that primary schools should not adopt a practice whereby each aspect of the curriculum is taught by the teacher specializing only in the teaching of that subject. We regard such a practice as likely to be disadvantageous for children between 3 and 11 or 12, as well as being unnecessary, extremely difficult to operate in large schools with anything like present staffing levels and quite impossible in medium sized or small schools.

9.21 Nor have we met anyone who wishes otherwise, though there does seem to be some misunderstanding among witnesses about what others think. Our impression is that the confusion comes in part from an indiscriminate use of the term 'specialist'. We have heard the word or derivatives of it used to describe a teacher's knowledge or interest; to describe a form of teaching organization of the kind outlined in the previous paragraph; to describe a partial form of that organization; and to describe the narrowing of a pupil's curriculum so that he or she concentrates on some subjects and omits others. The confusion may also arise from real differences of opinion about the balances of advantage between: (a) ensuring the coherence of the curriculum, and (b) the provision of sufficiently high teaching expertise; or between (x) progression and development of learning, and (y) pastoral concern and care for a child as a whole. Unfortunately the discussion is too often about only one side of the various issues to be balanced.

9.22 We hope that what follows goes some way towards clarifying the issues and may even provide a basis for consensus.

9.23 We begin from the assumption that most teachers in primary schools can teach most aspects of the curriculum to most of their pupils. We are satisfied that this view is supported by the evidence available to us, including what we saw on our visits to schools. It is particularly important that the younger children are provided for in ways that do not present them with frequent changes of teachers, though we are sceptical of the point of view that they are worried when other adults occasionally come into their classroom. In our experience a good many were delighted with the chance to show what they were doing or to ask about us. Moreover, in North-Rhine Westphalia where there is much 'half-time' teaching, two teachers often share a class with no sign of ill-effects on the children.

9.24 As we have already said, it is too much to expect every teacher to keep up with changes in knowledge and methodology in every field. Each would be helped by having a colleague nearby to turn to for information and help from time to time, and especially so if the roles of adviser and advised could be exchanged on other occasions i.e. that there was no question of hierarchy.

9.25 We envisage that the colleagues giving help should do so in two main ways: by taking the lead in the formulation of a scheme of work; and by helping teachers individually to translate the scheme into classroom practice either through discussion or by helping in the teaching of the children. Much the most frequent method would be discussion. Direct teaching might often take place with the class teacher present, not least so that the class teacher can manage on his or her own next time. But sometimes it might be better to teach the children away from their own teacher because that is easier for the coordinator to manage, or because to do so makes it possible to avoid distraction, or because the class teacher could use the time to do something else. If the teaching is done separately, the class teacher should be responsible for ensuring that the work done fits with the rest of the child's programmes. Linkage with the rest of the programme is what matters not where the teaching takes place. Children near the end of the primary stage are more likely to need access to additional teachers than are those near the beginning.

9.26 We believe this scenario represents the highest common factor of

> what various witnesses have put to us and is consistent with what we have seen and been told by teachers in schools. (House of Commons Select Committee, 1986)

It can be seen that the House of Commons Select Committee saw the way forward as a *development* of the then existing ways in which coordinators worked. The Committee clarified the role in a number of important ways (for example, the notion of the specialist, the effects upon the coordinator's class); and acknowledged the challenges facing class teachers, namely of trying to resolve issues of curriculum breadth, depth and balance. Nevertheless, the Committee accepted that primary schools should adhere to the class teacher system whilst simultaneously proceeding with coordinators. In effect the Committee made a persuasive case for coordinators and gave the notion of curriculum management and school development through coordination a powerful boost.

Soon after the Select Committee published their report, HM Inspectors published an interesting booklet entitled *Primary Schools: Some Aspects of Good Practice* (DES, 1987). This booklet describes the characteristics of schools where, in HMI's terms, good practice was observed. Some of these characteristics were cited in chapter 3 but, to briefly reiterate, they involved notions of: schools possessing a shared sense of purpose; teachers utilizing their individual curricular strengths to benefit the whole school; and the school's staff working as a combined teaching unit. The schools' aimed:

> . . . to ensure in all classes that the responsibility for coordinating the work of the class would remain with the class teacher and that, for the most part, the class teacher would teach much of the curriculum to that group of children, while at the same time, and where there was an advantage to the children, teachers with particular expertise in certain subjects might interchange classes or groups with teachers with strengths in other subjects . . . some teachers in these schools were acting effectively as consultants by helping to plan the work, and prepare the teaching materials. Some of these teachers were responsible for the development of a single subject, others had responsibilities which related to broader aspects such as project work . . . (DES, 1987)

Again the search for a balance between class teaching and coordination (or consultant as HMI called it) can be seen. Essentially, HM Inspectors, like others before them, were trying to weave into primary schools another organizational thread. To supplement the work of class teachers, coordinators were needed. This extra thread was needed because of the desire for schools to be 'whole' schools: in a sense class teachers were the weft, coordinators the warp. Together, they made the fabric of a whole school.

Coordination and the Whole School

We have already noted that HM Inspectors believe in schools becoming combined teaching units. Moreover, in chapter 3, we also advocate participation, and shared leadership. These ideas are generally consistent with the ideal of the 1980s: collegiality. Throughout the last ten years there have been increasing calls for schools to develop whole school policies, for teachers to collaborate and for the work of the school to cohere. Indeed, a new vocabulary appeared in respect of school and curriculum management (see, for example, Campbell 1985). In a 'whole' school it was said the curriculum should be:

continuous;
consistent;
coherent;
cohesive.

This would involve teachers and heads in many more *communications* and much *collaboration;* but the ultimate purpose would be to *coordinate* the work of the school. Several writers call this *collegiality* (see Richards, 1986; Thomas, 1987) although others are more sceptical (Campbell, 1985; Southworth, 1987; Open University, 1988). Whether all of this really amounts to a collegial organization must remain an open question because collegiality has not yet been adequately defined; nor do we have case examples showing us what collegiality actually looks like in a primary school. However, two things can be said. First, the call for whole school approaches relies, substantially, upon coordination. Schools will not become holistic without all staff being involved and without the work of the staff, both individually and collectively, being coordinated in some way or other. In short, calls for whole schools are cries for coordination.

Second, the desire for whole schools is really an acknowledgment that schools are prone to fragmentation. This was raised earlier in the context of the autonomy of class teachers. Individual and independent teachers have tended to be portrayed as creating the conditions for inconsistency and discontinuity. Coordination and collaboration have been prescribed as ways of reducing negative aspects of independence, yet, the negative aspects of collaboration (for example, cosiness; how time consuming it can be) have not been acknowledged. Neither have the implications of whole school management been appreciated.

The PSSR project (Nias, *et al,* 1989) suggests that whole schools are actively created. A whole school does not exist simply because staff attend meetings together or appear to demur about school aims. Rather, a whole school appears to be the product of many deep and overlapping school structures and processes. For one thing there needs to be agreement about educational beliefs: particularly the moral and social purposes of education; and what constitutes effective practice. Unless there is a working agreement on these matters fragmentation is more likely than cohesion. Also, schools need to come to terms with the tension between individuality and mutual interdependence. This point has been highlighted at various points (for example, class teachers and coordination) and is central to working arrangements in the school as an organization (see Ball, 1987; Nias *et al,* 1989). Next, schools need to devise ways of working which provide appropriate levels of communication, negotiation, and decision-making to support the school's development into a unitary whole. Crucially, schools will need to find ways of resolving differences in belief and practice which might exist between members. Such structures and processes are, in themselves, a challenge (sometimes obstacles) to the development of a whole school. However, they are attainable as the PSSR project shows (Nias *et al,* 1989), yet they appear to:

take time to develop;
are greatly influenced by heads and other leaders;
rely, in part, on opportunities to select staff;
need to be actively developed and sustained;
involve many staff — teaching, ancillary, secretarial and caretaking — working together.

Moreover, the PSSR project findings show that whole schools are founded upon, and consistently supported by, the school's culture, especially the 'culture of collaboration' (Nias *et al,* 1989).

In short, whole schools may require coordinators to play their part, but the attainment of a whole school is really the culmination of many structures and processes which, over time, have brought about the circumstances where staff can and do work together. Calls for whole schools may be cries for coordination, but coordination alone does not make a whole school. This can also be seen in the ILEA's 'Junior School Report' (1986; Mortimore *et al,* 1988).

The ILEA report offered a set of 'key factors of effective schools'.

Some have been noted in the previous chapter (pp.57,61) but it is worth listing all twelve factors:

1. Purposeful leadership of the staff by the headteacher
2. The involvement of the deputy head
3. The involvement of teachers
4. Consistency amongst teachers
5. Structured sessions
6. Intellectually challenging teaching
7. Work centred environment
8. Maximum communication between teachers and pupils
9. Limited focus within sessions
10. Record keeping
11. Parental involvement
12. Positive climate

In a sense coordination is embedded in all of these. Because an effective school requires the *presence* of all twelve of these factors, this will only be managed through coordination of effort (as points 1, 2, 3, 4, 10, 11 and 12 imply). Yet, coordination is not the sole attribute of effectiveness, so too is involvement (of staff and parents), structure and effective teaching and learning. Indeed, the twelve factors enable us to make some general points about the management of school development and the coordination of the curriculum.

It appears that school management needs to maximize attention to teaching and learning. Factors 6, 7, 8 and 9 imply that teachers in effective schools spend the great majority of their time working with children. This is, of course, obvious yet it needs to be stressed because schools, sometimes, are in danger of an imbalance between educational intentions and organizational ones. The former are concerned with how teachers teach, what the children are learning, how the curriculum is received and whether the children's work matches the school's aims. The latter consists of such things as the projection of the school's image (or reputation), links with the community, and neighbouring schools, and fund raising events. Whilst both need to be addressed educational intentions should exceed organizational ones. Unfortunately, in some instances, teachers can be distracted from imaginative teaching or reflection and sharing of insights about teaching and learning, by a rash of jumble sales, fetes, concerts and sponsored events!

Another point concerns the involvement of parents. Parental help in classrooms, educational visits and attendance at meetings to discuss children's work and progress had positive effects. So too was an 'open door' policy by heads to parents, and involvements in the children's school work at home (especially reading). It would appear that securing and maintaining the parents' involvement with their children's learning was beneficial both to the children and the school.

It is also worth highlighting three of the other listed factors (in addition to the three discussed in the previous chapter) because they relate more directly to the management of development:

> 4 **Consistency amongst teachers**
> It has already been shown that continuity of staffing had positive effects. Not only, however, do pupils benefit from teacher continuity, but . . . it appears that some kind of stability, or consistency, in teacher approach is important.
>
> For example, in schools where all teachers followed guidelines in the same way (whether closely or selectively), the impact on progress was positive. Where there was variation between teachers in their usage of guidelines, this had a negative effect. (ILEA, 1986)

This suggests that curriculum guidelines should be practical. It also implies that guidelines should be conceived not only as 'defensive' documents, that is as ways of demonstrating to those to whom the staff is accountable (parents, LEA, governors) that they know how to plan and design a curriculum, but also that guidelines are 'offensive'. That is, guidelines should affect positively, classroom practice and contribute to the combined efforts of the teachers (and other staff) as a school-wide unit. Similarly with record keeping:

> 10 **Record Keeping**
> The value of record keeping has already been noted, in relation to the purposeful leadership of the headteacher. However, it was also an important aspect of teachers' planning and assessment. Where teachers reported that they kept written records of pupils' work progress, in addition to the Authority's Primary Yearly Record, the effect on the pupils was positive. The keeping of records concerning pupils' personal and social development was also found to be generally beneficial. (*Ibid*)

Lastly, the ILEA report notes the importance of the school climate:

> 12 **Positive climate**
> The Junior School Project provides confirmation that an effective school has a positive ethos. Overall, the atmosphere was more pleasant in the effective schools, for a variety of reasons.
>
> Both around the school and within the classroom, less emphasis on punishment and critical control, and a greater emphasis on praise and rewarding pupils, had a positive impact.

> Where teachers actively encouraged self-control on the part of pupils, rather than emphasizing the negative aspects of their behaviour, progress and development increased. What appeared to be important was firm but fair classroom management.
>
> The teachers' attitude to their pupils was also important. Good effects resulted where teachers obviously enjoyed teaching their classes and communicated this to their pupils. Their interest in the children as individuals, and not just as pupils was also valuable. Those who devoted more time to non-school chat or 'small talk' increased pupils' progress and development. Outside the classroom, evidence of a positive climate included: the organization of lunchtime and after-school clubs for pupils; teachers eating their lunch at the same tables as the children; organization of trips and visits; and the use of the local environment as a learning resource.
>
> The working conditions of teachers contributed to the creation of a positive school climate. Where teachers had non-teaching periods, the impact on pupil progress and development was positive. Thus, the climate created by the teachers for the pupils, and by the head for the teachers, was an important aspect of the school's effectiveness. This further appeared to be reflected in effective schools by happy, well-behaved pupils who were friendly towards each other and outsiders, and by the absence of graffiti around the school. (*Ibid*)

This is consistent with the discussion in the previous chapter concerning leadership for participation and, especially, the creation of a collaborative culture as identified by the PSSR project (Nias *et al*, 1989). Moreover, it suggests that 'coordination' is not solely to do with the formal curriculum, but also with the informal (for example, conversation, after-school activities) and, perhaps, the so-called 'hidden' curriculum.

A number of points can now be made about the management of school development. For a number of reasons class teachers need to be supported in their work and the role of coordinators was designed to provide that support. During the last ten to fifteen years much has been learned about the role of the coordinator. The problems and successes of coordinators have been listed and are widely recognized. During the 1980s though, the role of the coordinator was further developed. Whilst support for class teachers remained as one expectation, coordinators came to be regarded as an important means of making the work of the school more cohesive and unified. Latterly, the PSSR and ILEA projects have shown that coordinators alone will not make a school a whole school. Creating a whole school is rather more complex than coordination and involves many processes (for example, leadership, teaching and learning, collaboration, culture, climate). Nevertheless, all the evidence points to primary schools relying heavily upon coordinators for their development. A tradition of school-based development has perhaps begun, and this tradition involves coordinators. It would seem foolhardy not to continue with the tradition since by so doing the insights gained from the experience of coordinators can be applied to school development. If coordinators were a major way by which the primary school curriculum developed during the 1970s and 1980s, how then might the experience be applied to further develop schools and curriculum? However, in asking this question we need to be aware that times have changed and there is a new context to face.

The New Context

All the evidence drawn upon has looked at the context before 1987/88. Yet the academic year of 1987/88 marked the beginning of a new period. During that school year new salary structures and conditions of service were introduced, and legislation was constructed for the introduction of a National Curriculum. The implications of these developments will be reviewed to see whether they mark the end of the coordinator's role.

The 1988 Education Act legislates for a National Curriculum. Moreover, it prescribes both curriculum content and the means for assessing children's learning of that content. Yet it does not appear to offer any advice as to how the tenets of the National Curriculum should be implemented. Furthermore, because the 1988 Act introduces a *National* Curriculum the legislation decreases LEA activity in curriculum design and planning and may actually place a greater responsibility on *schools* to install the proposals of the subject working groups. In other words, although a national curriculum assumes that the control of curriculum content will rest with central government, it also assumes that the prescribed curriculum content will be introduced at school level through school-based processes of curriculum implementation. Since school-based processes of development and implementation have previously relied upon the work of coordinators it is reasonable to assume that coordinators will continue to have a part to play in curriculum development. However, that part is now likely to involve a greater emphasis and attention to process issues as against content ones.

It also needs to be shown how the salary restructuring and new conditions of service introduced in 1987 do not necessarily adversely affect the notion of coordination. Two reasons can be offered. First, although most primary school coordinators were paid on scale 2 (pre-1987) and felt that the 1987 pay award brought an increase in salary but a loss in status, there are signs that several LEAs and individual schools have successfully introduced the idea that every teacher on the main professional grade is a coordinator for a designated curriculum area or part of the school. This is consistent with the House of Commons Select Committee Report (1986) as cited above (see p. 74-6). Second, whilst the salary restructuring has shaken the pre-1987 formal, hierarchical structure of primary schools (for example, scale 1, scale 2, deputy head) and 'flattened' that structure somewhat by removing a tier of promoted posts, it is more than probable that a powerful informal structure will remain. This informal structure relies on the fact that a person is rarely promoted for performing the basic tasks defined in his/her job. Rather, people are promoted for doing lots of additional things on top of the core duties of the job. For example, a main grade teacher may well not be promoted simply through demonstrating competence in the classroom. Instead, they are likely to be promoted for also demonstrating willingness to organize parental involvements in the school, ability to develop aspects of the curriculum and so on. Whether this is fair or right is not the question and, indeed, one should recognize that such a feature is potentially exploitative. Nevertheless, it is more than likely that such a structure will continue to work (as it has in the past) and as such it may entice teachers who wish to apply for incentive payment posts, or deputy headship, or who wish to change schools, to take on coordinating roles. Therefore, either formally or tacitly, coordinating tasks are likely to remain as an expectation of teachers on the main professional grade.

Lastly, the influence of tradition should be recognized. It was suggeted earlier that perhaps coordinators have now become an acceptable and traditional way of working in schools. If so then, like other traditions, they may be harder to stop and more resistant to change than some believe. Old habits die hard — and this might apply to coordinators.

Some Further Issues

If the way forward is to build on what we have learned from past experience and apply these lessons with greater vigour it seems necessary to highlight some of the likely issues.

First, coordinators will need to be more aware and skilled in respect of: curriculum implementation; the management of change; and curriculum evaluation (see chapter 5). This is because with the advent of a national curriculum attention to content will tend to decrease. At the same time, schools will be required to introduce, implement and review the proposals made by the subject working groups. Yet schools will remain involved with content issues since they will undoubtedly need to *interpret* the working groups' recommendations in the light of their own circumstances (for example, pupils' needs, school resources and materials, environmental factors etc.) and *translate* them into classroom practice.

Second, coordinators will continue to need to be skilled in working with colleagues. Since coordinators are still to play an important role in school development (either in terms of the National Curriculum or school-based initiatives) their role rests substantially on how effectively they can work with colleagues. Fortunately, Campbell (1985) has shown how coordinators have worked productively with colleagues and, in broad terms, has mapped out the sorts of skills they need (for example, social, representational, personal, leadership skills). Nor, should we forget that many coordinators already possess the necessary skills. Indeed, a positive feature of continuing with coordinators is that schools will benefit from retaining the existing large number of experienced and skilled teachers who have, and presently still are, doing the job. Nevertheless, further support is likely and in-service will have a major contribution to make.

Third, external support will be needed. The work currently conducted by advisory teachers, and ESG teams will remain as a valuable asset and continuing need. Yet, more will need to be learned and understood about how advisory teachers work effectively with schools (see Biott, 1988) so that both parties can mutually benefit and develop.

Fourth, we need to try to understand the ecology of school cultures, particularly those which foster collaboration and development. The work of the PSSR project, the ILEA project and those who study school effectiveness and school improvement should be brought to bear upon primary schools.

Fifth, the work of the headteacher needs to be carefully considered. What do heads need to do to support coordinators? How can heads best enable coordinators to make a significant contribution to school development? Some answers were offered in chapter 3 but it is crucial that heads consider such things as:

- providing time for coordinators to see work in other classes and with their colleagues throughout the school;
- enable coordinators to lead meetings and workshops;
- provide opportunities for coordinators to report to governors and parents;

- ensure that expenditure is planned so that coordinators have a budget to manage and can purchase where necessary, resources.

Just as with the deputy, such facilitation is not only the medium of development but also its message since colleagues will be aware that coordinators have status as well as responsibility.

Sixth, coordinators need to work with their colleagues, in each other's classrooms. A coordinator for language, say, will need to talk with colleagues. They also need to watch children at work in colleagues' classrooms: How do the children use books; what are they reading; what is their spoken language like at different ages; how are the children writing? The classroom must become accessible to coordinators. They need to see the children, and their colleagues at work. This is not to imply some inspectorial role, rather it is to allow coordinators to see the strengths of their colleagues, to witness the curriculum in action, and to begin to consider the child's received curriculum. For some time such activity will be essentially descriptive with the coordinator describing to a colleague what s/he has seen. It may then develop into a critical friendship. But the main point to recognize is that classrooms need to be more open so that teachers can see and share what they each do (see Pollard and Tann, 1988).

Seventh, coordinators will need to be coordinated. The work of any individual coordinator needs to be related to and fitted with work in other areas of the curriculum and/or school. Who coordinates the coordinators is an interesting question. As a general rule we believe it is a task many deputies could undertake.

These seven points are just the more obvious ones, and each is treated in only a relatively superficial way. Hopefully, individual schools will address them more fully and consider how they might respond. However, it might also seem that a great deal is being expected and that an overwhelming task is being prepared. Rather than see this as some daunting, grand design, we would encourage teachers to think of this as small scale, and 'doable'. All we advocate is what many schools have been doing for a long time. Moreover, if development is regarded as lots of little things, each done a little bit better, by everyone, then the combined effect is large and worthwhile. To achieve distinction does not require some sleight of hand by a single genius, rather it is about the commitment of all members to each do something a little bit better (see Peters and Austin, 1985). The only thing we would add is that all these little improvements need to be recognized, planned and evaluated which is why we are attracted to school development plans.

Already readers will be aware that school development requires attention to lots of different and diverse matters (for example, staff, children, parents, governors, resources, curriculum plans, evaluation, communication, leadership . . .). The coordination and management of all and each of these aspects rests upon the school having a plan for its development as chapter 2 argues and as the next chapter reinforces.

Chapter 5

Evaluation for Development

> Listening to one another and to themselves, they feel where the music is going and adjust their playing accordingly. They can do this, first of all, because their collective effort at musical invention makes use of a **schema** — a metric, melodic, and harmonic schema familiar to all the participants — which gives a predictable order to the piece. In addition, each of the musicians has at the ready a repertoire of musical figures which he can deliver at appropriate moments. Improvization consists in varying, combining, and recombining a set of figures within the schema which bounds and gives coherence to the performance. As the musicians feel the direction of the music that is **developing** out of their interwoven contributions, they make new sense of it and adjust their performance to the new sense they have made.

This quotation from Donald Schon (1983) describes the delicate interplay and complex webs woven by a jazz combo. Without stretching the point too far, it is possible to argue that this quotation is saying much about the role of evaluation in school development. The process framework — built around evaluative questions and described in chapter 2 — represents the underlying **schema,** which gives a basic shape to the enterprise. Evaluation techniques compose the **repertoire** — to be called upon to activate, and give body to, the schema. Put together, the schema and the repertoire of techniques create 'the piece', which **develops** out of the interwoven contributions of individuals, small groups and the whole 'band'. In applying their feel for the situation and in thinking about what they are doing, the members are, according to Schon, in the process **evolving their way of doing it,** i.e. mobilizing and developing the development culture.

The particular point, however, is that evaluation can provide the process schema and the technique repertoire; the **warp and the weft of school development.**

This chapter, then, aims to explore the role of evaluation in school development. It opens with an example of 'collegial evaluation' (i.e. collaborative enquiry) in action and then identifies three hallmarks of self-evaluation in schools: at best, it is a **learning journey** based on **staff involvement** and focussing on **classroom processes.** A piece of typical collaborative enquiry — involving paired observation — is then described and four implications drawn from the issues arising. It is a question of:

orchestrating and managing the change process;
providing a framework for development;
attempting climate analysis as part of the process;
establishing a collaborative support partnership.

There has been a consistent thread throughout this book thus far. This thread is **evaluation,** or, to be precise, **self-evaluation;** at various points we have described it as:

the **life-blood** of school development;
the **linkage** within the Developing School;
the essence of **collaborative enquiry**;
a **trigger mechanism** for mobilizing and energizing the development work;
the activities that provide **fusion** for the integrity required by the development culture.

Evaluation, then, underscores the Developing School.

The Developing School is the Evaluative School

At this point it is worth restating the case for evaluation in schools:

- Involvement in self-evaluation is now seen as a legitimate in-service activity. It can be a vital form of staff development and can provide the linkage between staff development, curriculum development and school development. This is the process of **fusion** mentioned above.
- By combining various evaluation approaches and techniques, it is possible to provide a **process framework** for school development. It becomes the vehicle for growth inside the school and a central component of the **development culture**; it provides the **internal capacity** for moving forward.
- Evaluation also provides the **vehicle for the transfer of**

ownership; through involvement in evaluation, the staff members become committed to the development of their school; and according to Goodchild and Holly (1989),

involvement generates commitment

When the 'baton' is passed to the staff within evaluative activities, their involvement takes the form of

collaborative enquiry

And, echoing another of the themes of this book, collaborative enquiry is a form of

participative learning for teachers

Some of these issues are touched upon by Roper, Deal and Dornbusch (1976) in their paper entitled 'Collegial evaluation of classroom teaching: Does it work?'. These authors were reporting on a **programme of work** which had three purposes:

(i) to conduct a programme of collegial evaluation (or collaborative enquiry) to improve classroom teaching;
(ii) to enable teachers to join together in partnerships for peer observation and conferencing. The focus of the work, therefore, was **paired observation** (see Holly, 1986b);
(iii) to monitor the impact of team-working on the process of organizational change;

The authors admit that the work entailed breaking the professional mould in two ways: it meant breaking down teacher isolationism in the classroom and it involved the learning of evaluation skills on the part of the teachers. As a consequence, the programme included an emphasis on open plan classrooms and team-teaching, plus skill training in evaluation. Given the 'open-doors' policy and the fact that,

> . . . the teaching performance is more visible under these conditions than in the traditional classroom, teachers viewed evaluation of their teaching by colleagues as more legitimate.

As evaluations were exchanged, teachers developed more respect for the ability of their colleagues to make sound judgments and were more willing to be evaluated.

By doing evaluation, they became more evaluative

Moreover, the evaluation work, conducted in the partnerships, consisted of seven interrelated steps:

(i) **finding a partner:** it proved important to build in friendship and voluntaryism as two 'principles of procedure' as the 'climate' of the pairing (revolving around the need for trust, respect, honesty, and supportiveness) was crucial;
(ii) **selecting evaluation criteria** — or performance indicators;
(iii) **self-assessment** (based on the chosen criteria);
(iv) **pupil assessment,** i.e. an evaluation of the teacher by the pupils;
(v) **paired observations,** based on an exchange deal within the pairings and using the chosen criteria;
(vi) **conferencing,** involving feedback and practical suggestions and the initiation of an 'improvement plan';
(vii) **improvement plans** to be finalized and implemented.

Roper *et al* (1976) identified two major problem areas in conducting work of this nature:

1 *The selection of criteria*
This proved a difficult task; the problem is the degree of specificity and precision built into the criteria. How exact and finely detailed can such criteria be? Is it good enough, they ask, to talk in terms of broad indicators? Some examples could be:

rapport with students
ability to motivate students
facilitates student participation in discussion

Are these specific enough? Despite this difficulty, however, one of the teachers in the programme was able to declare:

> Selecting useful criteria forced me to clarify my own educational philosophy. I had to decide what was really important to me and then try to operationalize my goals so they could be observed.

Yet experience in the GRIDS project would suggest that teachers are not used to doing this; selecting criteria for effectiveness is not, as yet, a common feature of classroom/school life. It could be argued, however, that it is a major professional responsibility.

2 *The level of staff involvement*
Roper *et al* (1976) emphasized that the evaluation scheme operated in the programme was suitable for (and, indeed, was implemented by) a whole staff, a teaching team or any two interested teachers. In this context, it is interesting to note the use of the terms 'collaboration' and 'collegiality' in North America. It seems that they are pressed into service to describe *all*

levels of joint involvement; therefore, two teachers working together on paired observation are described as being involved in a 'collegial' relationship. In the UK, however, it seems that the term 'collegiality' is reserved for use in describing more full-scale, wider staff involvement (see Coulson, 1976). The question which underpins this discussion is a vital one: which level of involvement in evaluation leads to school development; which level leads to holistic, as opposed to fragmented, reform? (see Holly, 1984).

Holly (in Southworth, 1987b) has pointed out that initiatives in the area of classroom self-evaluation (or action-research) have tended to lack any organizational bite, while the whole school approaches (such as GRIDS) have tended to lack impact in individual classrooms. What is needed, therefore, is an approach which succeeds in spanning both dimensions — the organizational (school) and the individual spheres (classroom) — and, thus, in using evaluation productively for school development. Holly (1986c), in the Teachers' GUIDE, amended the GRIDS format in an attempt to solve this particular problem; and it is the resulting process framework which underscores the conception of the Developing School contained in this present volume.

This framework has three hallmarks:

1 It uses various kinds of evaluative approaches to form a 'learning journey'; it is a process model which is both developmental and cyclical. Essentially, it is a question of combining in a sequential form.

    evaluation **as** development
    evaluation **for** development
    evaluation **of** development (see Holly and Hopkins, 1988)

  Once these 'processes' are placed within a cyclical structure, it is then a question of finding appropriate techniques to do the 'processing'.

2 The framework provides ample opportunities for the whole staff — or teams of staff members — to become involved, thus encouraging the transfer of ownership of the development work to the staff at large. **Ownership** is an interesting concept. According to the dictionary definition, it has two meanings: there is the sense of possessiveness (the sense that something belongs to you or that you identify with something) and there is the sense of the 'confessional' i.e. owning up to something. Self-evaluation, we would argue, can score on both points. It belongs to the staff — it is theirs — and it leads to the acknowledgment and recognition of, and attachment

Figure 10:

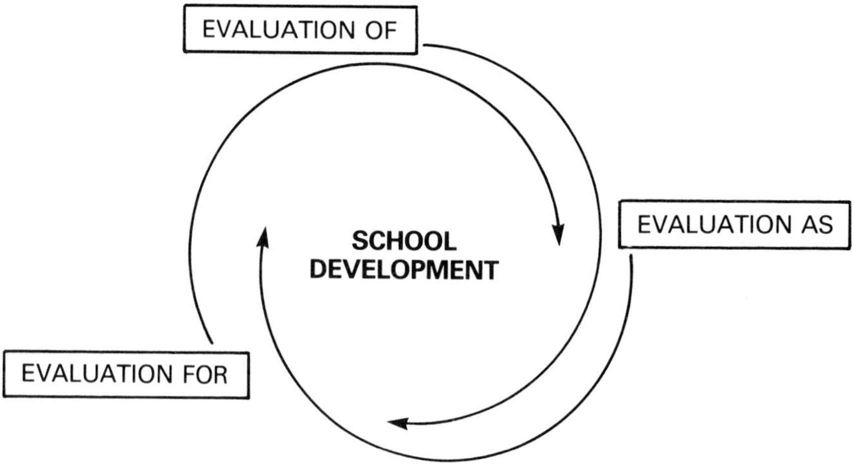

to, the issues requiring priority attention. It is a case of 'psychological affiliation' and of the generation of **self-confrontation.**

Collaborative enquiry, therefore, can become a (self-) critical dialogue between caring professionals; professionals who are reflective practitioners. Indeed, collaborative inquiry can be viewed as the work of a **reflective community.** Such a group of reflective inquirers needs to be both a **skilled community** (the members of which are able to make creative use of a repertoire of evaluation techniques on the one hand and have expertise in the skills of collaboration on the other) and a **focussed community** (involving the negotiation of a shared agenda).

Torbert (1976) described the efforts of the staff of one particular school to create a community of inquiry. It was, he said, a school trying to learn and

> transform itself into a real community of inquiry, a school trying to change in pace with its members' changing understanding of its mission and of their own needs.

This transformation, however, proved problematical to say the least. As a consequence, Torbert had two solutions for the problems encountered:

(a) the acquisition of the skills of collaboration to enable staff members to learn from their difficulties together, provide strength from within the school and energize growth and commitment.

(b) the organization of the whole school into a learning environment (i.e. a community of enquiry), so that it was more integrated, more adaptive and more effective. This is the central aim of Organization Development (OD), which constitutes an attempt to help schools

> . . . become more aware of their own processes and culture and thus gain more control over their own destiny.

According to Torbert, there are two ways into OD work in schools: the first involves intervention by external 'scholar consultants' who are invited into the school in question; the second is evolutionary and involves the internal generation of the development work.

It was Schaefer (1967), within his model of the 'school as a center of inquiry' who introduced the idea of a 'scholar-teacher', a lynch-pin role for the development of sustained school-university cooperation. Smith *et al* (1986) have offered a summary of Schaefer's analysis which, in turn, we have amended.

Figure 11:

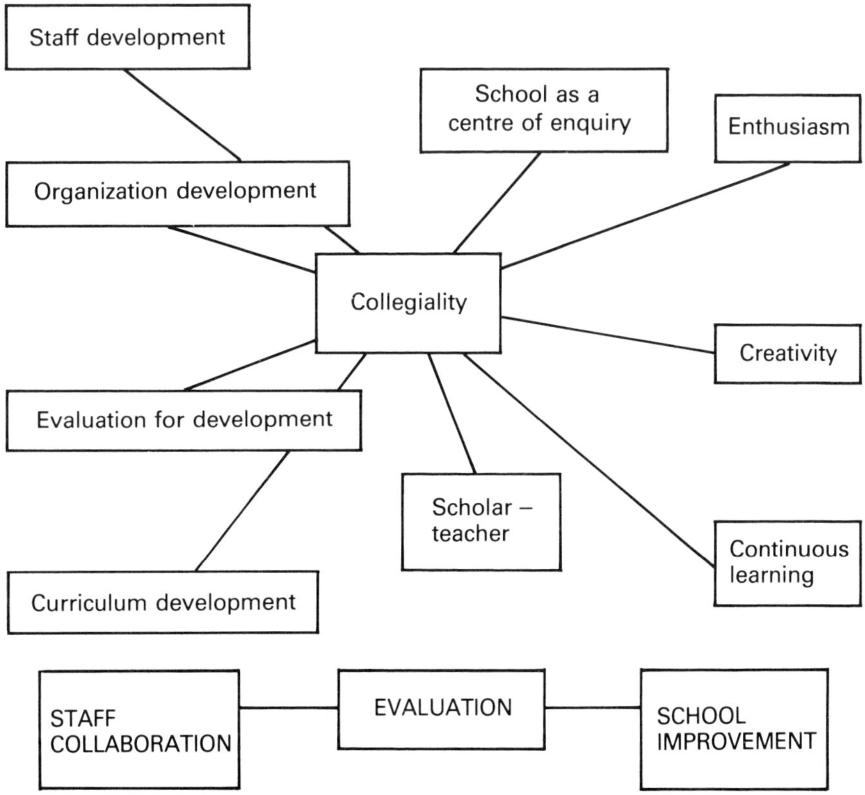

This diagram emphasizes that involvement in collaborative evaluation not only enhances the collegiality of the staff but also transforms the school into a centre of enquiry.

3 If the focus of the evaluation work remains **close to the proceses of teaching learning,** then staff collaboration becomes the linkage between the two domains — the school as an organization and the world of the individual classroom. This is particularly the case if the staff collaboration becomes a vital part of the culture of the school.

When these three characteristics are in combination, therefore, it becomes a matter of the staff collaborating in doing evaluations for the purpose of improving classroom processes across the school.

Keeping these hallmarks very much in mind, consider this scenario of school-based evaluation.

Paired Observation

Members of staff decided to investigate the teaching and learning styles being employed in classrooms across the school. They also decided that the initial vehicle for this investigation should be **paired observation.** A third of the staff volunteered to be part of this exercise and they were encouraged to team up with 'someone you feel happy working with'. Friendship groups were the norm. It was also agreed that mutual reporting would be incorporated into the scheme. Accordingly, the observations were conducted and the reports exchanged. All the reports were then collated and an external consultant was asked to analyze them and pick out the issues emerging from the reports generally. The next step consisted of a meeting of all the staff members involved during which the consultant fed back his analysis.

At one point the consultant mentioned that classroom 'noise' was an issue in many of the reports. Some members of staff said that there was 'too much noise'; others that there was 'not enough noise'; and still others that there was 'just about the right level of noise'. In responding to this, one staff member exclaimed:

> You've touched on a taboo subject. Noise is an issue in this school but it's never mentioned. Everyone knows that there's an implicit rule about the level of noise, but it's never been spelled out . . . We don't talk about it, but it's very important.

These comments led to general staff discussion concerning the connections between 'noise', 'excitement', 'creativity', 'control' and 'learning atmosphere'.

Following this session, it was decided to inform the rest of the staff of developments thus far. The significance of the general issues arising from the reports was discussed and, based on this dialogue, some agreements reached about the next stages in the review and development work.

Paired observation undoubtedly triggered the development process in this particular school.

Paired observation can be powerful because:

(i) observing the behaviour of other teachers may make a teacher aware of his/her own teaching;

(ii) it is a powerful learning experience in itself; it enables colleagues to share ideas;

(iii) teachers rarely see their peers teaching;

(iv) it helps to break down the 'psychological walls' between classrooms, thus eroding isolationism (see Joyce *et al,* 1983);

(v) it can be non-threatening, informal and non-judgmental; it can provide an opportunity for 'mirroring' in terms of the partner collecting information for his/her colleague to use in a self-evaluation;

(vi) within this kind of relationship, team-spirit, trust and collaboration can develop over time;

(vii) it is both child-focussed and teacher-focussed; indeed, it is **learning-focussed;**

(viii) it provides stimulation arising from discussion, reflection, analysis and collaborative action. (adapted from Sparks, 1983)

'In summary', says Sparks, 'peer observation — which 'equals' observing each other — seems to be a promising activity for staff development. To be most effective, however, it should occur in an atmosphere of trust and collaboration'.

In our view, the 'cameo' described above has much to say about the role of evaluation in school development. In particular, it reminds us of the importance of:

- the management of the change process;
- the orchestration of the development work in terms of finding a productive balance between evaluation processes and techniques; extending the learning (from evaluation) across the staff;
- climate analysis, i.e. getting under the skin of the school;
- the appropriate and timely use of external support agents; the use of a collaborative support partnership.

In the rest of this chapter we will focus on each of these four points in turn.

1 *Management for Change*

Bennis and Nanus (1985) emphasize the importance of 'getting it right'. It is a question of feel, intuition and educated experience; staff members edging their way forward by taking stock at every stage. It is very much a case of looking back to look forward — or, as Karl Weick has referred to it, 'retrospective sense-making'. In this context, it is useful to note that 'models' and 'frameworks' often take shape **after the event.** In this particular school, the shape of the development work gradually emerged over time; it was certainly not there at the beginning. It is often a case of 'starting small, but thinking big' (see Fullan, 1987).

2 *The Framework for Development*

Whether a framework is produced prospectively or retrospectively, it is vital in terms of structuring, guiding, mobilizing and synthesizing the development processes. Such a framework is built around the 'tension' between processes and techniques. This dynamic relationship is not only crucial for development, but also provides a variety of entry points. While processes need techniques and vice versa, entry into development work can be via the process or technique dimensions. Looking at the diagram below, it means that a staff could use paired observation as an entry point at one of several stages in the development process.

Figure 12 can be viewed as a set of process guidelines which, if used flexibly, might provide a 'road-map' across which to plot a suitable route for development. The model caters not only for a variety of starting points but also as a reminder of the reciprocal relationship between processes and techniques. As a result, the staff members can either work through the processes (and can select appropriate techniques along the way) or select a technique, apply it and, in taking stock thereafter, reflect on the process implications. Either way, the staff are continually working with, and within, the dynamic between the process and technique dimensions. As mentioned above, the model can be activated prospectively or retrospectively. It is also the case, however, that the staff need to be confident in selecting from a repertoire of evaluation techniques. A range of techniques has to be mastered (in training workshops), thus providing the staff with the opportunity of using a variety of techniques

Figure 12:

Key processes / Key techniques	GRIDS review sheet	Structured staff discussion	Staff interviews	Work shadowing	Paired observation	Interest group feedback session	Snowball session	Formulation of performance indicators
What do we need to look at? Identification of development needs					*			
Where are we now? Stock-taking; gathering evidence of present situation					*			
Where do we want to be? Target-setting								
How do we get there? Strategic planning; identification of INSET needs					*			
How are we doing? Monitoring and evaluation					*			

over time. Indeed, it has been argued that, within the change process, a combination of pressure (for change), a shared vision and **knowledge of the first steps** is powerful enough to overcome internal resistance.

In addition, there is some evidence that **confidence** in the application of evaluation techniques has another vital repercussion.

Teacher confidence is closely related to teacher empowerment; the one engenders the other. And there is some evidence that, through the **skilful** and **successful** use of evaluation, teachers gain in confidence, feel more empowered and look upon evaluation itself in a much more positive light (see Fullan, 1985; Guskey, 1986; and Holly and Hopkins, 1988). It is very much a case of doing evaluation **as** an in-service activity, coming to see its application **for** development and, eventually, realizing its potential for the monitoring **of** the effectiveness and impact of current changes. But it is a learning journey over time during which the teachers are gradually emboldened to move from 'evaluation as' to 'evaluation for' and, finally, to 'evaluation of'. As in all learning journeys, there is a great deal of unlearning to do (concerning perceptions of evaluation) before teachers internalize its importance. Eventually, however, within a climate of collaborative enquiry, teachers are ready to confront their practice and become professionally accountable. At this point the use of performance indicators — for the purposes of 'quality control' — will come into its own and the staff members will be able to match their observed, actual performance against the elements of their intended practice.

In terms of doing 'evaluation of', there are various approaches from which to choose. One possible way forward is to do a 'fidelity' study which consists of an investigation into the 'levels of use' of an innovation according to pre-determined characteristics of the particular innovation (see Hall and Loucks, 1977 and figure 13).

3 *Climate Analysis*

The open discussion — in which the staff became involved in the scenario above — triggered the talk of 'taboos' which implies that the staff are beginning to look at the culture of the school and, as Holly (1986a) has argued, one of the major tasks in school development is to analyze and regenerate the cultural dimension. But this is the most difficult task of all (see Heckman in Goodlad, 1987). It is so difficult that the way in is through the school's climate — the 'felt', perceivable, tangible aspects of the school's culture. Climate analysis, therefore, is an entry point. There are, however, two points to keep in mind:

Figure 13: Levels of Use of the Innovation

		Levels of Use of the Innovation
0	Nonuse	State in which the user has little or no knowledge of the innovation, no involvement with the innovation, and is doing nothing toward becoming involved.
	Decision Point A	Takes action to learn more detailed information about the innovation.
I	Orientation	State in which the user has recently acquired or is acquiring information about the innovation and/or has recently explored or is exploring its value orientation and its demands upon user and user system.
	Decision Point B	Makes a decision to use the innovation by establishing a time to begin.
II	Preparation	State in which the user is preparing for first use of the innovation.
	Decision Point C	Changes, if any, and use are dominated by user needs.
III	Mechanical Use	State in which the user focuses most effort on the short-term, day-to-day use of the innovation with little time for reflection. Changes in use are made more to meet user needs than client needs. The user is primarily engaged in a stepwise attempt to master the tasks required to use the innovation, often resulting in disjointed and superficial use.
	Decision Point D-1	A routine pattern of use is established.
IVA	Routine	Use of the innovation is established. Few, if any, changes are being made in ongoing use. Little preparation or thought is being given to improving innovation use or its consequences.
	Decision Point D-2	Changes use of the innovation based on formal or informal evaluation in order to increase client outcomes.
IVB	Refinement	State in which the user varies the use of the innovation to increase the impact on clients within the immediate sphere of influence. Variations are based on knowledge of both short- and long-term consequences for clients.
	Decision Point E	Initiates changes in use of innovation based on input of and in coordination with what colleagues are doing.
V	Integration	State in which the user is combining own efforts to use the innovation with related activities of colleagues to achieve a collective impact on clients within their common sphere of influence.
	Decision Point F	Begins exploring alternatives to or major modifications of the innovation presently in use.
VI	Renewal	State in which the user reevaluates the quality of use of the innovation, seeks major modifications of or alternatives to present innovation to achieve increased impact on clients, examines new developments in the field, and explores new goals for self and the system.

(a) The climate of a school is so pervasive, so all-embracing and so mundane, that it often goes unnoticed. It is the everyday atmosphere of the place; it is too familiar, too obvious. It is the taken-for-granted, **assumed** and unseen side of school life. There is a need, therefore, to render the 'familiar unfamiliar' and vice versa.

(b) The climate of a school is also something of a facade which is used to camouflage and mask the potential of cultural (i.e. value) difference. As Biott (1988) and Holly (1986a) have contended, it is easier — organizationally speaking — not to 'rock the boat'. It is the realm of **value of difference passivity.** For development to occur, however, the cultural values at work in a school may well have to be investigated and analyzed — to be disturbed. But it is a delicate task. As Biott (1988) has said, such a process must be constructive as opposed to destructive.

Finlayson (1973), Moos (1974) and Fraser and Fisher (1983) have all suggested ways of doing climate analysis using various kinds of School Climate Scales (see below). Sirotkin (in Goodlad, 1987) has described the process of critical enquiry, which, he says, is an attempt to monitor the 'health' of a school and to provide the staff with enough evidence for informed action. It is, he argues, a case of gathering information concerning the **context and setting** of the school, its **internal processes** and the **meanings** by means of which the staff members make sense of their working world. Data collection in these areas allows for the diagnosis of the 'health' of the school and could take the following forms:

- still photographs or videos of the school in action — to be discussed by the staff in terms of their symbolic qualities;
- interviews with 'key informants' concerning the history of the school; the dreams, aspirations and values of its 'shapers' and 'builders'; and typical stories of the school's priorities, commitments and ambitions in action;
- classroom/school observation such as work shadowing (of staff members), pupil pursuits, and 'A Day in the Life', which Sagor (1981) has claimed is a technique for assessing school climate and effectiveness. The sample given below is the 'product' of a team of observers shadowing eight children. Techniques, of course, can also be used in combination and the 'Day in the Life' strategy could be linked with the basic questions from 'Curriculum in Action' (see below)

What did the pupils ACTUALLY do?

What were they learning?

How worthwhile was it?

What did the teacher do?

What did the teacher learn?

What should the teacher do now?

These questions are adapted from the Schools Council/Open University course P234 'Curriculum in Action' which is a Continuing Education course for teachers.

- mapping devices like the example included below:

'Day in the Life' Checklist and Observers' Findings

Taking this school day as a whole, do you feel the student would have:

	YES	NO	Undecided or No response
1. Felt the school had high expectations for his/her achievement?	2	5	1
2. Felt the climate was orderly and conducive to learning?	5	2	1
3. Felt the instruction provided was based on data regarding his/her understanding? (Monitoring)	4	2	2
4. Felt the instructional materials made available were appropriate to help him/her learn?	5	1	0
5. Felt his/her good school work and effort were appreciated?	5	3	0
6. Felt his/her day was structured to provide the maximum opportunity to learn? (Academic learning time)	2	6	0
7. Felt most of his/her class time was spent productively and on task?	2	5	1
8. Felt the school was dedicated primarily to the process of learning?	3	3	2
9. Felt he/she was an active participant in the teaching/learning process?	3	3	2

PRACTICAL ACTIVITY 11.1

Aim: To describe a school ethos.

Method: Rate the school on the mapping device below (derived from Rodgers and Richardson, 1985, pp.52-3). Ask some colleagues to do the same and discuss the results.

	1	2	3	4	5	
busy						inactive
happy						miserable
purposeful						aimless
relaxed						tense
enthusiastic						apathetic
noisy						quiet
messy						tidy
chaotic						organized
welcoming						formidable
open						closed
disciplined						unruly
confident						insecure

Follow-up: Use of the mapping device, and the conversations with colleagues which follow, should provide a good idea of the subjective feel of the school. An excellent extension would be to ask children, parents or non-teaching staff to carry out the exercise too. They are likely to have different perspectives. All sorts of issues for school practice and provision might follow if particular patterns emerge from the exercise.

Many commentators agree that a school's culture has a vital role to play in the change process (see Holly and Wideen, 1987; Sarason, 1971; and Deal and Kennedy, 1983). As Holly (in Goodlad and Holly, 1989) has argued, the stronger, more stable, and more affective a school's culture becomes, the less inclined the school is towards innovation. Innovations are potentially destabilizing; as a consequence, every innovation is filtered and screened by the culture of the school. The business world has woken up to this same phenomenon. Recent newspaper headlines, for instance, have included these examples:

> How 'company culture' can be carried too far
>
> Company culture shock
>
> How 'company culture' can block innovation

Heckman (in Goodlad, 1987), however, has concluded that

> those interested in improving schools confront the culture of the school and the problems involved in changing the culture . . . Goodlad and Sarason (have) proposed that the very cultural concepts that help explain lack of change could be employed by school-based groups to produce change.

In other words, the culture that so often works against change initiatives can be marshalled in support of change, i.e. the development culture (see also Joyce *et al,* 1983). Heckman refers to the 'renewing culture' as 'healthy' and capable of promoting the incorporation of new ideas into teachers' current perceptions and practices. Like Sirotkin and ourselves, Heckman sees **collaborative enquiry** (involving external support and an investigation of value differences) as the way forward and lists five enabling characteristics:

> principal/headteacher leadership
> staff cohesiveness
> a 'take-care-of-business' attitude
> staff problem-solving process
> adequate assistance

Like Holly (1984), Heckman was puzzled by research findings which highlighted the difficulty of achieving both organizational and classroom changes:

> It appeared that teachers in more renewing schools engaged in problem-solving activities together and subsequently solved school-wide problems but they did not attend together very much to what they did behind their classroom doors. This is interesting and puzzling because teachers and students spend most of their school time in classrooms. It could be argued that school renewal should be related significantly to what goes on in classrooms. The hard rock issues manifest themselves in classrooms . . . The puzzle opened up somewhat, however, as we examined additional data in which we saw another trend . . . **teachers in most schools remain isolated from one another.** They do not discuss very much what they do in their classrooms. They do *not* discuss significant classroom problems and seek collegial solutions to them . . . They spend little time talking substantively to one another about what they do in their classrooms . . . Schools have cultural regularities that promote this isolation. Teachers, on the average, teach alone. They spend most of their school day alone in their classrooms with people who are not their peers.

Given this dilemma, Heckman and Holly have offered the same solution: collaborative enquiry linking the individual and organizational dimensions.

Collaboration, then, is the key; and a partnership for collaborative enquiry, which focusses on ways to renew both the school as an organization and the classrooms across the school, is the way forward. In essence, says Heckman, what is required is an investigation of the 'entire culture of the school . . . teachers and principals promote renewal when they solve school problems together'. Indeed, Heckman's solution is very similar to the stance taken by ourselves earlier in this chapter. He poses four questions to be considered by a staff investigating a particular area of the curriculum — in this example, mathematics (see below). Heckman's suggestions remind us of the task to be fulfilled by a 'specific review team' operating within the GRIDS process guidelines. Indeed, one particular GRIDS team came up with a scheme which involved them in:

(i) filing a review of current practice;
(ii) formulating criteria for 'worthwhileness' — the internal view;
(iii) ascertaining criteria for 'worthwhileness' — the external view;
(iv) merging the fruits of (ii) and (iii) to the team's satisfaction;

(v) compare this new 'map' with present practice (as filed) and recommend an action plan to reduce the distance between the two.

Stage One **Teachers describe together *what* they do**
The idea is to focus on an area of, say, mathematics teaching in terms of:
- teaching strategies
- learning activities
- materials which they characteristically use

Stage Two **Teachers discuss together *why* they engage in these characteristic practices**
The idea is to begin to ask questions of the routine practice:
- why use worksheets so much?
- what conceptions of maths guide this activity?
- what conception of worthwhile maths is reflected in these activities?

Stage Three **Teachers work out what additional information is required**
The idea is to collect evidence of good practice in maths and statements of worthwhileness
- what is available in the research literature?
- where can we obtain useful, relevant knowledge?

Stage Four **Teachers match this new knowledge (containing a view of effectiveness) against their present practice**
If there is a mismatch, what action should we take?

(vi) attention to be paid to the complexity of the classroom;
(vii) the collaborative research to be both rigorous and useful.

What these features amount to is a fundamental change of relationship between those inside and outside the school. It is a question of doing interactive research and development on behalf of classroom teachers. In her own work, Lieberman has discovered that the support roles can be played by a variety of people; and collaborative research can be accomplished in a variety of settings, can enhance professional development and can focus on all kinds of concerns. As Lieberman concludes,

> participation in the process as a member of a collaborative research team is a powerful means for teachers to establish greater collegial relations with other teachers.

Figure 14:

The five stages of the internal review and development process

STAGE 1 GETTING STARTED

1 Decide whether the GRIDS method is appropriate for your school.

2 Consult the staff.

3 Decide how to manage the review and development.

STAGE 2 INITIAL REVIEW

1 Plan the initial review.

2 Prepare and distribute basic information.

3 Survey staff opinion.

4 Agree upon priorities for specific review and development.

STAGE 3 SPECIFIC REVIEW

1 Plan the specific review.

2 Find out what is the school's present policy/practice on the specific review topic.

3 Decide how effective present policy/practice actually is.

4 Agree conclusions and recommendations arising from the specific review.

STAGE 4 ACTION FOR DEVELOPMENT

1 Plan the development work.

2 Consider how best to meet the various in-service needs of the teachers involved in the development.

3 Move into action.

4 Assess the effectiveness of the development work.

STAGE 5 OVERVIEW AND RE-START

1 Plan the overview.

2 Decide whether the changes introduced at the development stage should be made permanent.

3 Decide whether this approach to internal review and development should be continued or adapted.

4 Restart the cycle.

5 Decide if you wish to inform anyone else about what happened in the first cycle.

Collaborative enquiry, then, enhances collegiality and leads to 'products', i.e. changes in classroom practice. Lieberman extends this point by usefully summarizing the benefits of such work:

The Benefits of Teacher Collaboration Teams for Research and Development

- Collaborative research and development creates a structure for teachers that facilitates reflection and action on the messiness of teaching and schooling problems.
- The team unites teachers and encourages collegial interaction. It has the potential for encouraging greater professional talk and action related to teaching, learning, and school problems.
- Both the process of group interaction and the content of what is learned narrows the gap between 'doing research' and 'implementing research findings'. The research question and the collection of evidence runs concurrently with plans for development of other teachers.
- Naturally occurring problems that teachers have in their schools may lend themselves better to this type of research and development than large-scale funded research, as it can respect the time lines of the school people rather than the research grant.
- A collaborative team provides possibilities for teachers to assume new roles and exhibit leadership. Feelings of powerlessness can be transformed into a greater sense of empowerment.
- Collaborative research legitimates teachers' practical understanding and their definition of problems for both research and professional development.

Lieberman's work described here has concentrated on in-school teacher groups aided by one or two external support agents acting as facilitators and co-learners. For effective school-based development, however, the support has to be more thorough-going, more systematic, yet more responsive within the 'all-hands-on-deck' mentality, there needs to be an external support infrastructure (see Holly, James and Young, 1987), which matches in style and approach the internal staff collaboration. What is being advocated here is a working partnership in support of school-based development. Such a partnership could include LEA staff, particularly advisers, advisory teachers and teachers' centre leaders, support agents from high education and external consultants generally.

Facets of the support partnership are as follows:

- collegiality is the corner-stone of the partnership both inside and outside the schools;
- it is very much a local partnership;
- what is required is both quality and quantity of external support;
- linkage is important: local networking, clustering and 'consorting' are very much part of the partnership; negotiation is a key concept.

Figure 15:

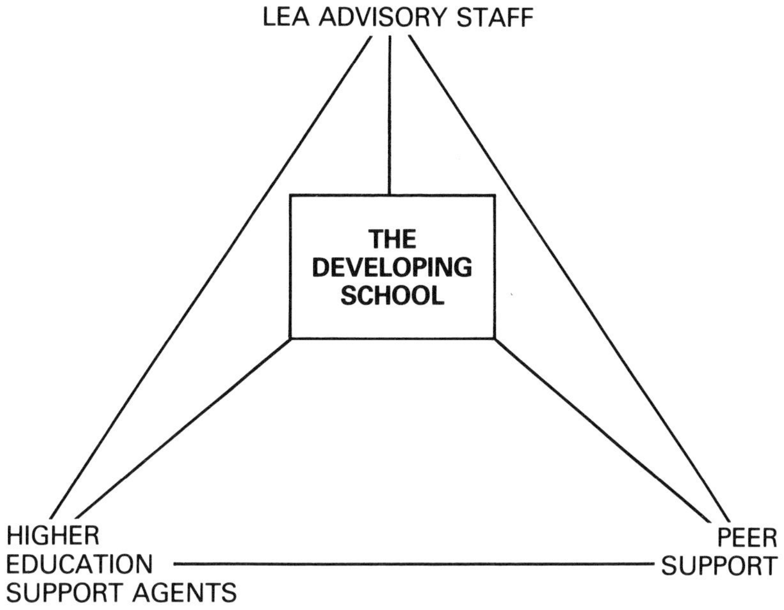

In addition, Holly, (1989) has listed some of the roles to be performed by external support agents. They included:

process consultant
content adviser/specialist
critical friend
link-person; coordinator
hands-on 'coach'
trainer
moderator
fixer; enabler and facilitator
co-research

Eisner (1985) has underlined the importance of the contribution of such an external agent:

> Teachers are too close; a critical friend provides a fresh eye, distance and an illuminative intent. Trust is crucial for a meaningful dialogue between teacher and critic; this is not quite coaching, more a counsel of friends . . . One makes oneself vulnerable only to those who one believes are not intending to hurt. Joint reflection rests on the investment of time in the classroom and an integrated process of professional development.

The establishment of an external support infrastructure is not only a major innovation in its own right, but also carries with it profound implications for training. Training, that is, for all those involved, whether they are internal or external to the schools, who have to identify and therefore incorporate existing strengths and skills, be prepared to use old skills in new ways and acquire new skills to be added to the support repertoire (see Holly, 1989).

Biott (1988) has worked with in-school coordinators and identified some of their on-going needs:

> At this time of increased interest in collective, school-based INSET, and especially in view of its promotion through GRIST, it seems appropriate to emphasize that coordinators of collaborative enquiry in schools will need continual support.

Indeed, says Biott, those trying to bring about collective learning in their schools should themselves be willing to learn about their task within a group of fellow coordinators; it is a case of doing (external) collaborative enquiry about (internal) collaborative enquiry. In addition, Biott has usefully listed some questions which collaborative groups can ask of themselves and their enquiry:

Criteria for Reviewing Progress

(i) Has the group begun to share a language which is encouraging, supportive and analytical?

(ii) Is the group engaged in the interpretation of actual evidence which is equally available to all participants?

(iii) Is involvement voluntary and not stratified according to organizational hierarchies, and are all viewpoints in the evidence, including children's comments, treated equally?

(iv) Are the enquiries empowering for participants?

(v) Have the enquiries led to people wanting to do things as a result?

(vi) Does the school-based enquiry group welcome the participation of outsiders in its work and do members seek opportunities for learning experiences in other settings?

(vii) Does the group wish to present its work to other audiences?

Biott (*ibid*) concludes:

> None of the above can be achieved mechanistically from an instruction manual. Those who have tried to sustain group learning will be aware of the 'fits and starts', the false leads, the troughs and the sideways drift. Some problems are anticipated at the outset, but most emerge later. Our future stock of knowledge

> of what collaborative enquiry means will depend on those with practical experience of it. Those LEAs sponsoring school-based INSET will probably find that the establishment of support groups for its coordinators will be money well spent. It will help to shape the future work in the schools and in the LEA. It will also help to build the kind of knowledge the profession urgently needs.

Collaborative enquiry outside the school can lead to the same work inside the school. Above all, says Sirotkin (and echoing one of the central themes of this present volume), evaluation, by disappearing into the mix of school development, becomes school development:

> School improvement must take place in schools *by* and *for* the people in them . . . and this process is not a one shot deal but an ongoing part of the daily worklife of professionals involved in their own school improvement efforts . . . In this context, evaluation becomes the process of rigorous self-examination, indeed the process of 'school renewal' itself.

Another vital element which disappears into the mix of school development is **staff development.**

Chapter 6

Staff Development

This chapter explores four aspects of staff development. The first is its linkage role in terms of blending school-focussed INSET opportunities with school development. We will argue that this has not always been the case, but that, with 'TRIST' and then 'GRIST' and now 'LFM', a quiet revolution has been occurring. As one observer commented recently, 'the world (of INSET) has moved on'. The second aspect is a set of characteristics which, when acting in combination, make for effective and impactful staff development. Here we are indebted to the research findings arising from the TRIST initiative and to the DELTA project in particular. The third aspect, which builds on the second, is the question of the integration of staff development endeavours within school development. Here we are indebted to the seminal work of John Goodlad and Ann Lieberman. The fourth aspect of staff development is its reliance on the quality of the organizational context or 'setting' in which it occurs. School receptivity is a crucial concept and may prove the vital factor in transforming staff development exercises from school-focussed activities into genuine school developments. The pioneering work of Bruce Joyce and his associates is given rightful prominence in this section.

Overall, however, this chapter is concerned with the ways in which schools can capitalize upon INSET opportunities and 'make them unto themselves'.

Like self-evaluation, staff development is a building-block, indeed one of the foundation stones, of the Developing School. To be able to fulfil this vital role, however, staff development has come a long way.

Holly, James and Young (1987) have charted recently the development of staff development. Ranged alongside professional development (i.e. the long-term process of enhancement of the practitioner's professional — classroom — performance) and career development, staff development (the enhancement of the practitioner's role as a member of staff) has grown in stature and importance the more it has become linked with school development. By and large, staff development is now synonymous with school development, because the staff are the major resource in the Developing School.

The recognition of the changing face of staff development, however, has been a gradual process (see below).

Figure 16: Important stages within the cumulative 'climate of ideas' in the U.K.

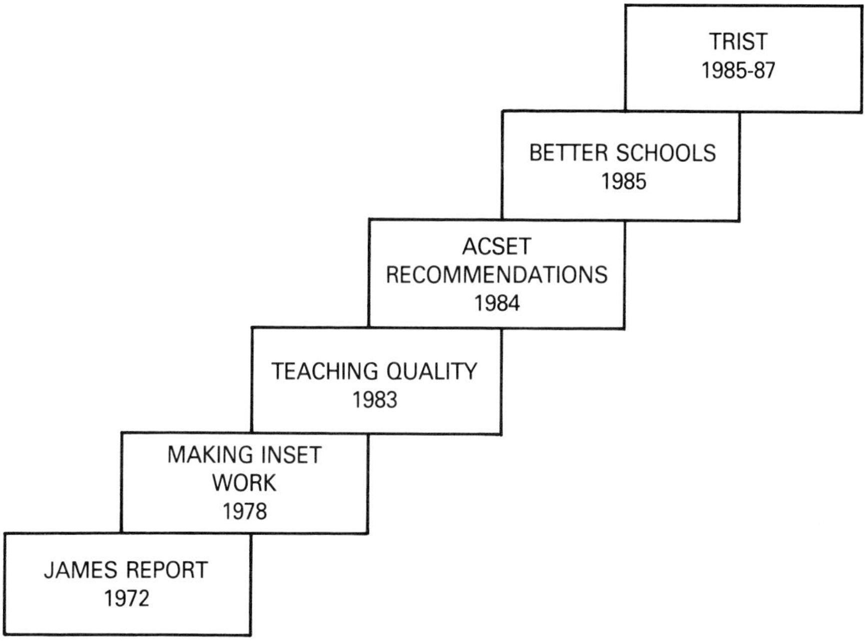

From the *James Report* onwards — including the seminal publication *Making INSET Work* published in 1978 — school-based/school-focussed INSET has steadily increased in popularity; so much so, in fact, that within TRIST (TVEI-Related In-Service Training) (see Holly, James and Young, 1987) and even more so within GRIST, school-focussed INSET has become the dominant mode of in-service provision. And, at best, school-focussed INSET is largely the same animal as staff development:

This, of course, has not always been the case. Writing in 1978, Rubin, in recording the greater importance being attached to in-service training generally, was also able to list some of its failings. According to Rubin, it was often far 'too lofty' (as opposed to dealing with fundamental classroom skills); 'too prescriptive' (thus ignoring teachers' needs, strengths and working contexts); 'too vague'; 'not useful' (lacking in practical application and conducted in isolation from the children — the very people whom it is ultimately supposed to serve); too faddish (too related to 'temporary fads' and not to the ongoing, basic problems of the classroom world); incapable of making up for the rapid obsolescence of initial training; and, to complete the indictments, generally not 'effectual', i.e. it does not lead to improvements being effected in the classroom. In other words, he argued, INSET has not made a difference:

> Humans tend to survive whatever does not cause them too much bother, and seemingly, the futility of most in-service education has not been much of a bother.

Indeed, it has been said that

> There is evidence to suggest that the more in-service training is institutionalized, the remoter it becomes from its addressees — the schools. (Block *et al,* 1983)

Rubin, however, in concluding that any 'attempt to improve children's learning depends on some form of teacher growth', was able to view positively the rise of the school-focussed movement. Indeed, his signposts for the future development of INSET included the following:

- Greater attention will be given to the practical applications of theoretical principles.
- Much more emphasis will be placed on locally-determined programmes that have maximum relevance.
- In-service education will become a more routine aspect of professional life.
- Quality teaching will be viewed as more important than the development of new curricula.
- Incentives will rely on the intrinsic rewards of superior craftmanship.
- Continuing professional education will be more collegial in nature (focusing on the interchange of ideas among experienced teachers) rather than perpetuating the traditional, leader-participating relationship.
- The uniqueness of each school mandates some latitude in the adaptation and use of techniques: therefore, new procedures in in-service programmes will be less prescriptive and more flexible.
- Diversity in both the organisation and methodology of staff development activities will be greatly enlarged, since all aspects of professional competence cannot be dealt with through any single mechanism.
- The participants in continuing professional development activities will play a major role in determining content, structure and process, as

well as in assessing the strengths and weaknesses of INSET programmes.

- The consultants, advisers, specialists and trainers in the in-service programmes will have a high degree degree of practical experience. They will be especially adept at cooperative interaction with professional teachers, and will be drawn from the ranks of the profession itself.

The school-focussed orientation of this list is unmistakable. Rubin would undoubtedly agree with the sentiments expressed by Skilbeck (1976):

> The best place for designing the curriculum is where the learner and the teacher meet . . . The teacher must look again at the situation he and his pupils are in, the learning situation, the social situation of the school, the context in which his activities are carried out . . . Cultural change asks teachers to learn new ways of thinking and behaviour and to acquire new skills and attitudes at the same time as it seeks structural or organizational changes.

Learning is where the school is.

If some commentators were beginning to see the way forward, however, in-service practice still lagged way behind. In his paper entitled 'Development of staff in primary schools (some ideas and implications), Southworth (1984) identified four 'models' of staff development:

(i) the 'systems' approach which determines staff development needs from an organizational perspective;
(ii) the 'laissez-faire' approach which allows each and every teacher 'to do his/her own thing'. Holly (1984) has referred to this free-for-all situation as the 'cult of the individual';
(iii) the 'pragmatic' approach which equates the credentialling process of INSET with career advancement and promotion;
(iv) the 'self-evaluative' approach which encourages teachers to reflect on classroom practice — individually and collaboratively. According to this model, staff development becomes a 'process' gain.

According to Southworth (like Rubin), the fourth model described here was 'emergent' and not 'prevalent' like the other three models. Indeed, more recently, Hargreaves (1988) has listed the shortcomings of in-service provision. It is

- uncoordinated and unsystematic (although some headway is now being made under GRIST);

- probably going to the wrong people, i.e. the volunteering, 'heavy consumers'. This results in inequitable distribution;
- largely unevaluated in terms of long-term effectiveness and impact in the classroom;
- person-centred not institution-centred;
- offered externally to institutions and does not become 'internalized'.

And, as Hargreaves has emphasized, school-focussed INSET is now seen as the vehicle for remedying these shortcomings. Heckman (in Goodlad, 1987) has underlined the importance of INSET being focussed on the school and geared to the needs of the school:

> When renewal and change efforts focus on the school, change efforts move away from large-scale in-service days for all teachers and in-service credit courses or workshops focussed on non-school problems. Indeed, district and other efforts encourage each school to focus on its problems and solve them as the teachers together use knowledge to create alternatives.

School-focussed INSET, when defined in these terms, is synonymous with staff development and, indeed, school-based development itself. As Hargreaves (1988) argues, the devolution of funding for INSET and the formulation of School Development Plans are two examples of the new deal for staff development. They both entail INSET activities servicing the needs of school development; and this means that INSET is fast becoming a built-in as opposed to 'bolt-on' operation.

While TRIST proved the turning point for many secondary schools, Holly and Martin (1987) have acknowledged the relevance of this experience for primary schools. As Holly, James and Young (1987) have argued, TRIST provided a host of opportunities to realize the new deal; and, by grasping these opportunities, those involved in TRIST discovered that INSET has to be:

established
applied
supported
evaluated
integrated

1 **Establishing INSET** has three aspects:

- establishing the foundations of INSET which, in TRIST, meant widening its scope, making it more accessible and increasing the scale of involvement, thus causing a tremendous upsurge in enthusiasm for, and participation in, school development activities by an increasingly large proportion of teachers (quoted in Holly *et al*, 1987);

- establishing the importance of INSET in the eyes of the teachers. Certainly the professional treatment of INSET in TRIST added to its status, its dignity and its credibility;
- establishing (i.e. identifying) INSET needs which proved a vital activity within the school-focussed orientation of much of the TRIST work. This process of the identification of needs involved local **brokerage** and **negotiation,** both crucial concepts.

Of course, within GRIST activities (interestingly referred to in some areas as 'Primary TRIST'), this process of establishing INSET has been extended to the primary sector.

2 **Applying INSET** involves rendering INSET more applicable, more relevant, more practical, more responsive and more meaningful. The central concept here was **targeting,** i.e. matching the needs of teachers and schools with more *focussed* INSET opportunities. This proved highly motivational as far as the participants were concerned, especially when they received appropriate and relevant provision which was obviously tailored to their expressed needs. In this context, negotiated and participative learning can be equated with more individualized learning for teachers. In other words, participating teachers (as learners) will have different needs at different times and INSET should be matched to, and congruent with, these differences. It is this matching process which gives rise to **Applied INSET** (see below).

Furthermore, many commentators have listed some of the factors contributing to effective in-service training. Hopkins (1986), Wade (1985), Sparks (1983) and Wood and Thompson (1980) have all listed some of the common properties of effective INSET. Wood and Thompson, for instance, have described the fruits of research on staff development; and their guidelines read very much like Applied INSET. Adults, they say, learn best through concrete experiences where they apply what is being learned and in informal situations where social interaction takes place. Like Holly (1987), they argue that 'experiential learning . . . maximizes the transfer of learning from the training setting to on-the-job application'. Wood and Thompson (1980) are able to conclude by listing six practical suggestions:

(i) include more participant control over the 'what' and 'how' of learning;

(ii) focus on job-related tasks which the participants consider real and important;
(iii) provide choices and alternatives that accommodate differences among participants;
(iv) include opportunities for participants in in-service training to practice what they are to learn in simulated and real work settings as part of the training experience;
(v) encourage participants to work in small groups and to learn from each other;
(vi) reduce the level of threat by enabling peer-participants to provide feedback.

Figure 17: The 'Matching' Process

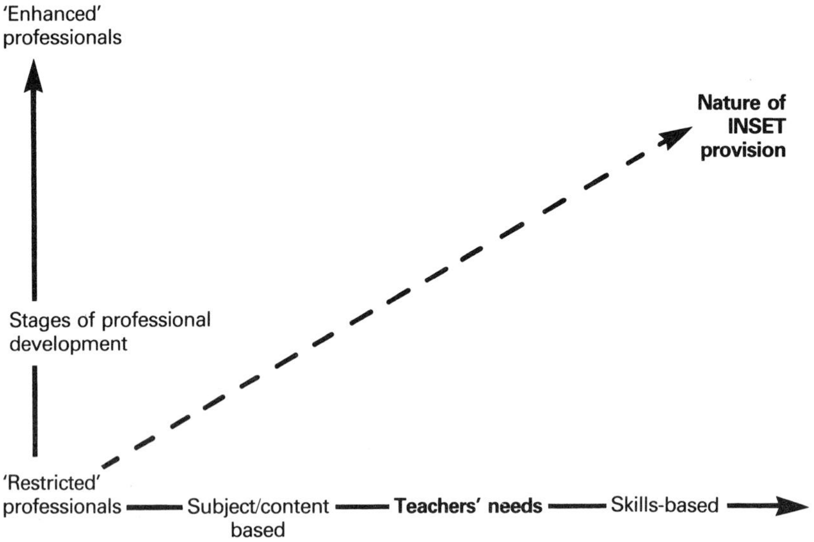

Joyce and Showers (1982) have included the concept of **coaching** in their list of elements of effectiveness. Coaching, they argue, is the vital link between the learning of skills and their classroom application. It embraces the provision of companionship; the giving of feedback; an analysis of when to apply the new ideas; adaptation to the needs of the children and the facilitation of ongoing, improved classroom practice. But coaching comes at the end of the INSET chain. Elsewhere, Joyce and Showers (1980) list the components of training process:

presentation of theory; awareness-raising;

> **modelling;** demonstration for concept acquisition;
> **practice through simulation;** skill acquisition;
> **feedback** (on the simulated practice), for example, micro-teaching;
> **coaching;** classroom application, on-going support and 'aftercare'.

Referring to the work of Joyce and Showers, Sparks (1983) points out that 'coaching could be provided by administrators, curriculum supervisors, college professors, or teachers'. Peer coaches, she adds, may be in the ideal position to provide the necessary 'hands-on, in-classroom assistance with the transfer of skills and strategies to the classroom'. Indeed, Sparks has summarized the work of the likes of Wood and Thompson and Joyce and Showers and come up with ten indicators of effective INSET:

(i) select content that has been verified by research to improve children's learning;
(ii) create a context of acceptance by involving teachers in decision-making and providing both logistical and psychological support;
(iii) conduct training sessions (more than one) two or three weeks apart;
(iv) include presentation, demonstration, practice, and feedback and workshop activities;
(v) during training sessions, provide opportunities for small-group discussions of the application of new practices and the sharing of ideas and concerns about effective teaching and learning;
(vi) between workshops, encourage teachers to visit each others' classrooms, preferably with a simple, objective, student-centred observation instrument. Provide opportunities for discussions of the observational work;
(vii) develop in teachers a philosophical acceptance of the new practices by presenting research and a rationale for effectiveness of techniques. Allow expression of doubts and let other teachers convince 'resisting' teachers through their 'testimony';
(viii) lower teachers' perceptions of the cost of adopting new practice through a 'nuts and bolts' approach;
(ix) help teachers grow in their self-confidence and competence through encouraging them to try only one or two new practices after each workshop;
(x) for teaching practices that require very complex thinking skills, plan to take more time, provide more practice, consider activities that develop conceptual flexibility.

Applied INSET, then, makes for effective INSET.

3 **Supporting INSET** was the cornerstone of school-focussed INSET in TRIST. The conception of a **support infrastructure** grew apace, with emphasis being placed on vital roles such as in-school coordinators/professional tutors ('a pivotal role', said one participant in TRIST), advisory teachers, providers and 'brokers', etc. In addition, with its 'staff-centred, locally-based and teacher-led' orientation, TRIST witnessed the growth of consortium-working and local (and, indeed, regional) coordination. It is, of course, the support infrastructure which has to be triggered in order to respond to the need for ongoing, in-classroom assistance for improving teachers.

4 **Evaluating INSET** was a 'growth industry' during TRIST. Evaluation **as** INSET, evaluation **for** INSET and evaluation **of** INSET were all accentuated. Evaluation was seen as an important INSET experience in its own right, as a formative service for the improvement of INSET activities and as an investigation of the effectiveness and impact of INSET. The need to do evaluations of the effectiveness of INSET was largely a reaction to the dispersal model of much of TRIST (including its financing); and, given the close connection between Local Financial Management (LFM) and school-focussed INSET, this will doubtless increase in importance.

Rubin (1978) has listed nine indicators (or 'professional criteria') to use when evaluating the effectiveness of in-service activities, which schools need to keep in mind and apply within their in-service arrangements:

(i) Are they relevant and appropriate?

> Teacher complaints of meaningless and irrelevance in in-service education programmes have been acknowledged in spirit and ignored in practice.

(ii) Is there flexibility of response or too much prescription?

(iii) Are they targeted (i.e. do they have clarity of purpose?) or are they imprecise, random and fragmented?

(iv) Are they practically relevant?

- are they too isolated from children's learning and the reality of classrooms?
- are they too 'lofty' in conception/not fundamental enough?
- are they too 'faddish' and not addressing real classroom problems?

(v) Are they cooperative and collaborative? Are teachers encouraged to educate one another?

(vi) Are they heading towards professional development?

- is there an ongoing, process orientation?
- is 'career-long development' being emphasized?
- is it a question of teacher re-education in terms of enhancing the repertoire of skills (fine-tuning) or learning totally different approaches?

(vii) Is the experience gained **making a difference** at whatever level in the school?

- individual classroom practice?
- team practice?
- whole staff/school practice?

(viii) What is the style adopted within the training? Does the medium match the message of the content? Is there congruence?

> In a curious way the training of teachers often violates many of the canons that we hold sacred in the training of students. Put bluntly, the methods used in in-service education have been for the most part, bad educational practice.

(ix) Are the differential needs of the participants being catered for? Rubin's contention is that all too often the 'typical programme presumes that all teachers are precisely the same in background, belief, knowledge, technical finesse, and teaching style'.

Fenstermacher and Berliner (1985) have also provided a rather sophisticated approach to the evaluation of staff development. They talk in terms of judging the INSET experience in terms of its worth, success and merit.

Worth constitutes the intrinsic worthwhileness of the chosen area of focus and activity

Success involves the achievement of intentions according to these five conditions:

- Did the **objectives** have sufficient clarity?
- What was the **quality of the instruction?**
- What was the **congruence** between the needs of the learners and the nature of what was provided (and learnt by the participants).

- What was the **applicability** of the learning experience?
- What was the **duration** (of practice) necessary for mastery of the newly acquired skills?

Merit concerns the quality of the learning process in terms of four aspects:

Sensibility: did the experience constitute a sensible use of time and talent?
Variability: for how long will the newly acquired 'skills' be used?
Incentive: what is the 'pay-off' for the learner teacher?
Maintenance: what collaborative support is available to sustain the learner? 'Maintenance' is similar to the concept of coaching.

By using such criteria as those mentioned above, a new view of evaluation is being promoted which countenances:

- the importance of the longer-term, process view of INSET as a part of the continuing education of teachers;
- the more needs-based, consumer-centred approach to INSET, involving targeting and increased negotiation between providers and teachers.

5 Integrating INSET

Holly (in Reid, Hopkins and Holly, 1987) has argued that the whole school can be both the recipient of, and the bulwark against, any wider learning arising from the INSET experience. Bolam (in Hopkins, 1986) has reminded us of the series of studies into the process of change at the school level carried out by the Rand Corporation in the USA. McLaughlin and Marsh (1987) have summarized the implications arising from this research through staff development and have concluded that the latter is critically influenced by organizational factors in the school. And it is this question of the organizational context which has concerned us in this present volume. We are not alone.

In a challenging series of articles and books, John Goodlad has explored the influence of a school's organizational context. Recalling the diagram posited in chapter 1, Goodlad (1972) has argued that, traditionally there has been an almost 'myopic' preoccupation with the 'monocultural' relationship of individual teacher and his/her pupils and their learning outcomes. 'Meanwhile', he said,

> the general context of schooling within which experiments are conducted, which probably has a great deal to do with what is happening to the students, remains unchanged . . . We often

> merely tinker when more fundamental examination and re-habilitation of the organism is called for.

In an attempt to rectify this imbalance, Goodlad, in the late 1960s, was instrumental in establishing the League of Cooperating Schools, the aims of which were to:

- initiate and sustain continuous school improvement;
- provide for a more healthy, more productive school culture in each of the schools by encouraging decentralized decision-making, the forging of new relationships and collaborative group-working;
- support the concomitant in-service growth of teachers both as individuals and as 'total faculties' (i.e. whole staffs);
- actively involve other constituents of the local partnership — or 'responsible parties' as Joyce *et al* (1983) refer to them — in launching into concerted, collective action;
- create a 'hub' (for example, an in-service agency or higher education establishment) to service the needs of the 'consortium' as a 'social system';
- use **networking** within this new social system to provide protection against the more 'conservative' expectations of the community and to combat the conception of innovation as tinkering 'around the edges' in order to make fundamental changes.

Goodlad's vision is very similar to our own — as we have tried to describe it in this book. His 'continuous improvement' is our development culture. And when he acknowledges that change has to be enacted at the cultural level, he is acknowledging not only the power of the culture of the school but also the fact that the staff members largely perpetuate the culture through their daily affirmation of its central tenets. If the staff 'make' it, they can undo it — by working in different ways and thus subscribing to other cultural values. Innovation without cultural change, therefore, is innovation without change. Additionally, and this has been a constant theme in this present volume, the staff need to decide upon a new mission — or **ethos** — in which are embedded new cultural values; then relate to each other in new and different ways, i.e. the **climate** of collaboration; and, finally, implement the changes at the deep cultural level — the classrooms across the school, which constitute the lived, informal **culture**.

Goodlad has this to say on these matters:

> By collective action these parties, of which the principal and

> teachers constitute the group most naturally accountable, must define the school's mission. There is a school culture which emerges, for better or worse, whether or not such processes occur — a culture which can be molded to a set of beliefs; a culture which deeply affects and should be shaped by all who are included in it. To be healthy, this culture must be sensitive to those within it and attuned to the conditions and events surrounding it . . . The project sought to focus on the culture of the school as central to both understanding and effecting educational change. The individual school was assumed to be the organic unit for change and a network of cooperating schools was created to provide a new social system committed to change. This social system legitimized and created a press for change . . .

This 'press for change', then, comes from in and around the participating schools. Such self-improving schools (the schools are the **improvers;** no longer the **improvees)** create new demands and new resources for staff development.

According to Goodlad, there are three central goals for staff development:

- First, the initial goal of staff development is, he says, to refine the school's process framework. In his work the framework was called DDAE (dialogue, decisions, actions and evaluation). The staff, he says, will need training in operating such a framework. But this is a far cry from the traditional situation in which 'staff development . . . meant in-service education for the individual teacher . . . the teacher has been regarded as important to the virtual exclusion of other factors'. It is these other factors which are now demanding the attention of staff development.
- Second, another goal of staff development is to produce guidelines and criteria for promoting, monitoring and evaluating the process framework. This is, then, a second order activity. Such criteria might include: the quality of group interaction; the extensiveness of the use of background reading and research; the planning of staff meetings (including debriefings); the conduct of small group meetings; and the quality of change leadership exercised in the school. The application of such criteria involves **staff development as evaluation of staff development.**

And according to Goodlad, these second order concerns, have a direct influence on first order activities. By coming up with and using evaluative criteria embracing a vision of good practice, the staff are led to emulate these criteria in their daily work. Consequently,

> (in the programme) total school faculties and sub-groups more and more imposed upon themselves the processes implied by their own criteria. School improvement and staff development became virtually synonymous.

- And third, there is the goal of collegiality as a process outcome of staff development. Teachers are encouraged to be collaborative and to offer each other mutual support within an institution which caters for a balance of interests and which is capable of sustaining itself in a healthy state. For Goodlad, as for ourselves, staff collaboration is the key for school improvement.

It is interesting to note that Ann Lieberman was a member of the League of Cooperating Schools and thereafter, in the 1970s and 1980s, she has written a series of definitive articles on the ins and outs of staff collaboration. Her latest work with Ellen Saxl and Matthew Miles (see Saxl, Lieberman and Miles, 1987) has concentrated on teacher leaders as staff developers. Reflecting on the increase in leadership opportunities for teachers, they point out that

> staff development is a natural outlet for teacher leadership, particularly in the delivery of school-site services.

They see such teachers as acting as 'professional assisters' in school improvement programmes:

> These programmes often depend on special 'assisters' who act as consultants, facilitators and staff developers. However, these individuals are often new in their roles, with inadequate training and support for the complex task of supporting school change efforts.

In fact, Saxl, Lieberman and Miles have been able to identify eighteen necessary skill areas (see below) and have built training modules to help to build these skills and the confidence to use them. These modules are clustered round the basic skill areas — the tools for the job — and are composed of five stages:

assessment of own skill level;
awareness-raising towards a deeper understanding;
skill development involving simulated practice;
application to on-the-job situations;

evaluation and feedback.

'It is our belief', they conclude, 'that teachers can make a significant contribution to staff development, either on a part-time or full-time basis, but ongoing training and support are a vital part of the process.'

All commentators, however, come back to the question of the power of the setting or organizational context in which staff development activities take place. Schools — and their levels of receptivity — make or break change initiatives. And staff development constitutes a change initiative.

Key Skills for Educational Assistance Personnel

Skills and Description	Examples
1. **Interpersonal Ease.** Relating to and directing others.	Very open person; nice manner; has always been able to deal with staff; knows when to stroke, when to hold back, when to assert; knows 'which buttons to push'; gives individuals time to vent feelings, lets them know her interest in them; can talk to anyone.
2. **Group Functioning.** Understanding group dynamics, able to facilitate team work.	Has ability to get a group moving; started with nothing and then made us come together as a united body; good group facilitator; lets the discussion flow.
3. **Training/ Doing Workshops.** Directing instruction, teaching adults in systematic way.	Gave workshops on how to develop plans; taught us consensus method with 5-finger game; prepares a great deal and enjoys it; has the right chemistry and can impart knowledge at the peer level.
4. **Educational General (Master Teacher).** Wide educational experience, able to impart skills to others.	Excellent teaching skills; taught all the grades, grade leader work, resource teacher; has done staff development with teachers; was always assisting, supporting, being resource person to teachers; a real master teacher; much teacher training work.
5. **Educational Content.** Knowledge of school subject matter.	Demonstrating expertise in a subject area; showed parents the value of play and trips in kindergarten; knows a great deal about teaching; what she doesn't know she finds out.
6. **Administrative/ Organizational.** Defining and structuring work, activities, time.	Highly organized, has everything prepared in advance; could take an idea and turn it into a program; good at prioritizing, scheduling; knows how to set things up.
7. **Initiative-Taking.** Starting or pushing activities, moving directly toward action.	Assertive, clear sense of what he wanted to do; ability to poke and prod where needed to get things done; had to assert myself so he didn't step on me.
8. **Trust/Rapport-Building.** Developing a sense of safety, openness, reduced threat on part of clients; good relationship-building.	In 2 weeks he had gained confidence of staff; had to become one of the gang, eat lunch with them; a skilled seducer (knows how to get people to ask for help); 'I have not repeated what they said so trust was built'; did not threaten staff; was so open and understanding that I stopped feeling uneasy.
9. **Support.** Providing nurturant relationship, positive affective relationship.	Able to accept harsh things teachers say, 'It's OK, everyone has these feelings'; a certain compassion for others; always patient, never critical, very enthusiastic.
10. **Confrontation.** Direct expression of negative information, without generating negative affect.	Can challenge in a positive way; will lay it on the line about what works and what won't; is talkative and factual; can point out things and get away with being blunt; able to tell people they were wrong, and they accept it.

11. **Conflict Mediation.** Resolving or improving situations where multiple incompatible interests are in play.	Effected a compromise between upper and lower grade teachers on use of a checklist; spoke to the chair about his autocratic behaviour and things have been considerably better; able to mediate and get the principal to soften her attitude; can handle people who are terribly angry, unreasonable; keeps cool.
12. **Collaboration.** Creating relationships where influence is mutually shared.	Deals on same level we do, puts in his ideas; leads and directs us, but as peers; doesn't judge us or put us down; has ideas of her own, but flexible enough to maintain the teachers' way of doing things too.
13. **Confidence-Building.** Strengthening client's sense of efficacy, belief in self.	She makes all feel confident and competent; doesn't patronize; 'You can do it'; has a way of drawing out teachers' ideas; injects a great deal, but you feel powerful; makes people feel great about themselves; like a shot of adrenalin boosting your mind, ego, talents, and professional expertise.
14. **Diagnosing Individuals.** Forming a valid picture of the needs/problems of an individual teacher or administrator as a basis for action.	Realizes that when a teacher says she has the worst class, that means 'I need help'; has an ability to focus in on problems; picks up the real message; sensitive, looks at teacher priorities first; knows when an off-hand joke is a signal for help.
15. **Diagnosing Organizations.** Forming a valid picture of the needs/problems of the school organization as a basis for action.	Analyzes situation, recognizes problems, jumps ahead of where you are to where you want to go; anticipates problems schools face when they enter the program; helped us to known where we should be going; helped team look at the data in the assessment package.
16. **Managing/Controlling.** Orchestrating the improvement process; coordinating activities, time, and people; direct influence on others.	Prepared materials and coordinated our contact with administration and district; is a task master and keeps the process going; makes people do things rather than doing them himself.
17. **Resource-Bringing.** Locating and providing information, materials, practices, equipment useful to clients.	He uses his network to get us supplies; brings ideas that she has seen work elsewhere; had the newest research, methods, articles, and ideas and waters them down for our needs.
18. **Demonstration.** Modelling new behaviour in classrooms or meetings.	Willing to go into classrooms and take risks; modelling; showed the chair by his own behaviour how to be more open.

Source: *Journal of Staff Development (1987), Spring, 8, 1, p.9.*

Sparks (1983), Joyce and McKibbin (1982) and Berman and McLaughlin (1976) have all stressed that staff development takes place within an organizational context and that this context has the power to determine its success (or failure). Moreover, Lieberman and Miller (1981) have argued for the effectiveness of supportive principals as 'instructional leaders', while Little (1981) has explored the subtleties of the relationship between the prevailing climate, the dominant mode of interaction and the school context.

Joyce and McKibbin (1982), in differentiating between 'growth states' of teachers ('omnivores', active consumers, passive consumers, resistant, and withdrawn), points out that there are enormous differences in the ability of teachers to pull **growth-producing experiences** from their environments.

> The interaction of teacher personalities can make or break school social systems, which, in turn, foster or inhibit teacher growth . . . it is virtually impossible for the formal system of a school whose informal system operates at a survival level to be open and permeable.

Joyce and McKibbin, like Holly and Goodchild (1989), differentiate between a school's formal and informal systems (or ethos and culture) and maintain that

> Schools with weak formal systems and negatively oriented informal systems operate under conditions that work against change . . . The informal social system is a powerful determining factor.

The same authors add that the relationship between the formal and informal systems (and, indeed, the quality of each) determines the school's energy level, its *receptivity* to change initiatives and the ability of negatively-oriented 'gate-keepers' to restrain (and even ridicule) their more enthusiastic colleagues. Indeed, say Joyce and McKibbin, the combinations of these factors produce organizational 'states' similar to Maslow's levels of 'needs' — self-actualization, comfort and survival — in a more collective sense. As a result, they are able to refer to three school scenarios.

Scenario One — The 'Self-Actualizing' School

This involves a highly energized, positive school environment — the result of a combination of a relatively powerful formal system and a solid and affirmative informal system. It is a case, say Joyce and McKibbin, of a school with open and strong formal and informal systems which activate the energies of individual members of staff. Such a school has the following characteristics:

free and strong interchange of ideas — with some ideas being trawled from the outside, considered with seriousness and taken on their merits;
considerable energy being expended on self-development;
warm, informal interchange which fosters more growth — producing activities by individuals, small groups and the staff as a whole;
change efforts are supported by the strong, formal system of the school;
the school has a strong, formal in-service programme which caters for both institutional and individual needs;

advisory, support staff are deployed effectively, so that they can interact productively with staff members.

Scenario Two — The 'Comfort' School

According to Joyce and McKibbin, such a school has a semi-positive orientation; any change efforts tend to be fragmentary rather than integrated or holistic in inspiration; it is

> 'supportive but not synergistic'

In other parts, there is energy being expended, but not in a whole-school, collective sense.

Scenario Three — The 'Survival' School

This is the kind of school which Joyce and McKibbin refer to as 'depressant', meaning one which has a negative environment and which generates obstacles to the release of energy. Such a school has a weak formal system and has a negatively-oriented informal system which operates under conditions that work against change. This kind of school is characterized by:

considerable less activity;
individual members of staff who feel that they have to be covert about their personal efforts, their isolation thus cocooning them from the ridicule of 'colleagues';
'phobic reactions' to the possibility of change.

Joyce and McKibbin (1982) conclude that members of staff create and are created by the social systems — both formal and informal — of their schools. In the terms used by Joyce and McKibbin, staff members 'are both affected by and part of (these) social systems'. In the pursuit of more healthy, self-actualizing schools, these authors 'urge the consideration of two strains of staff development . . . Both involve attention to the improvement of the social system'. One strain is Organization Development (OD) — as recommended by Torbert (1976) — and the other is

> the development of personnel as social therapists, skilled in creating a new social system, understanding it, helping individuals in it create a system oriented toward self-actualization.

What this all means, of course, is that, although 'characteristics of individuals are always, to some extent, a reflection of the setting in which these characteristics were manifested' (Sarason, 1971), these same individuals have the potential power of joining together — in collaboration — to create a new climate of relationships and, thus, a new 'setting' or organizational context. According to Nias, Southworth and Yeomans (1989), collaboration involves the interdependence of the individual and the group — for the enrichment of both. It is a question of maintaining both autonomy/enterprise and dependency.

Autonomy/enterprise	Valuing individuals as people
	Valuing individual contributions to the group
	Valuing interdependence: a sense of belonging to the team
	Valuing interdependence: working as a team with a sense of mutual dependence
Dependency	Accepting mutual constraint

Collaborative relationships, then, establish a new (interactive) climate which, in turn, links the new formal system with the school's informal system. Collaboration is the cornerstone of the new team approach to staff development. Collaborative staff development, therefore, like collaborative evaluation/enquiry, provides much of the vital linkage for school development.

Figure 18:

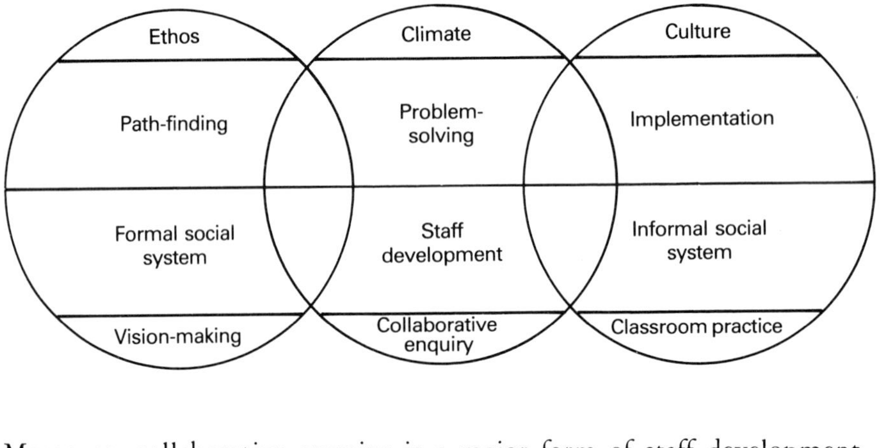

Moreover, collaborative enquiry is a major form of staff development. Indeed, Fullan (in Hopkins, 1986) has argued for:

- the need for in-service/staff development to be integrated with, and part and parcel of, concrete changes and problems experienced at the classroom and school level;
- within such programmes, staff training should be intensive and ongoing;

- the ongoing process of professional development should be linked to organization development efforts;
- teachers may well be the best source of skill and practical training, although external consultants should be used for particular purposes;
- above all, a plan is required at the school level, which systematically organizes and provides for the process of integration, i.e. the identification of staff development needs within a school development plan.

This last point reminds us that in-service needs flow out of institutional needs. Staff development planning is a cobbled together, fragmented affair until it is applied to the rationale established by the school's priorities for development. It is also the case that doing a School Development Plan is a staff development exercise in itself. As with

Figure 19: The developing school

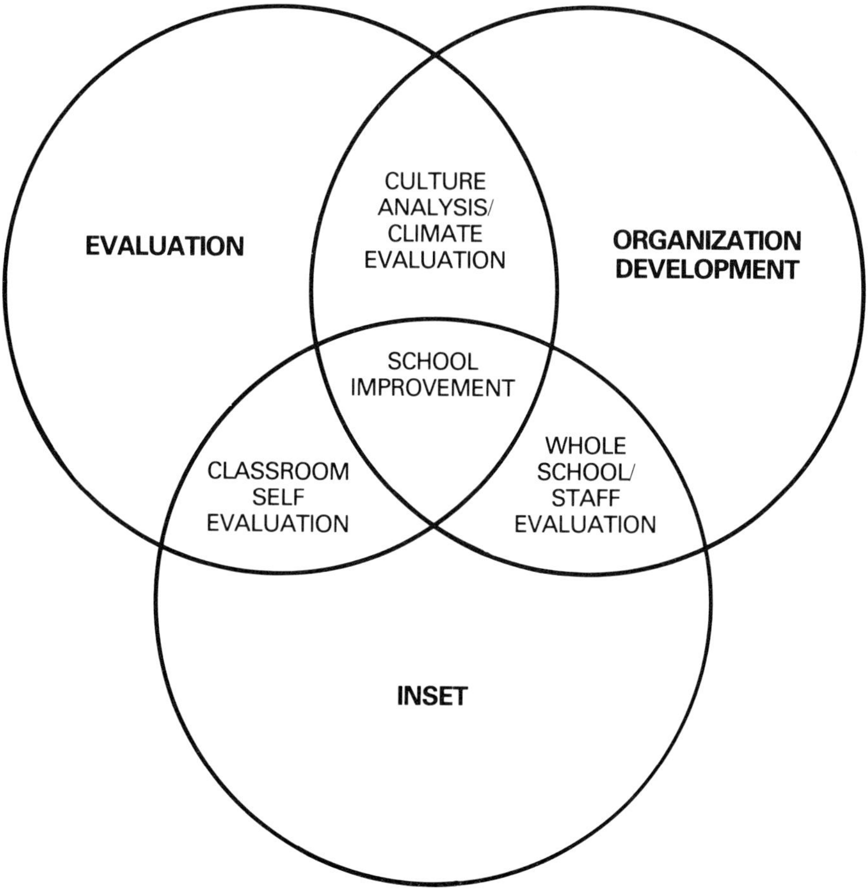

evaluation, staff development is such an integral part of school development that, at its best, it disappears into the mix of The Developing School.

Chapter 7

School Development: Making it Happen

> We trained hard . . . but it seemed that every time we were beginning to form up in teams we would be reorganized. I was to learn later in life that we tend to meet any new situation by reorganizing; and a wonderful method it can be for creating the illusion of progress while producing confusion, inefficiency and demoralization. (Caius Petronius, AD 65)

School development has to become habitual. It is a question of combining **continuous improvement** with the resolve to be 'regularly irregular'. As Cuban (1987) has pointed out, school development is a somewhat curious amalgam of **constancy and change.** Going against the grain becomes part of the grain. Fullan's advice (1988), therefore, is to get into new habits, especially the habit of constant learning. He advises schools to:

reach out and gain access to new ideas;
practise active experimentation;
examine other organizations;
encourage and support reflective practice;
establish collegial learning;
build in coaching in relation to classroom practice.

Fullan's emphasis on the importance of both reflective practice and coaching echoes the arguments put forward by Schon (1987) and Block (1987). Indeed, Fullan (1988) draws our attention to the concept of 'enlightened self-interest':

> . . . enlightened self-interest is the goal of simply learning as much as you can about the activity that you're engaged in. There's pride and satisfaction in understanding your function better than anyone else and better than even you thought

> possible. One of the fastest ways to get out of a bureaucratic cycle is to have as your goal to learn as much as you can about what you're doing. Learning and performance are intimately related; the high performers are those who learn most quickly.

Fullan builds on this passage and reaches three conclusions, all of which are vital to an understanding of school development:

(i) given the constant bombardment on schools of demands for change, what has to be avoided is **random learning;**
(ii) what is essential is a **critical screen,** or sifting mechanism, to make learning (and development work) more focussed and more purposeful;
(iii) healthy organizations (in a non-rational world) do not just happen; they become healthy through the efforts of their members:

> Organizations do not get healthy by themselves, and we all would be extremely lucky if our organization got healthy through someone else's efforts other than our own. Managing in a non-rational world means counting on our own selves.

And Fullan concludes his 'thought-piece' for headteachers/principals in resounding fashion:

> Paradoxically, counting on oneself for a good cause in a highly interactive organization is the key to fundamental **organizational change.** People change organizations. The starting point is not system change, or change in those around us, but taking action ourselves. The challenge is to improve education in the only way it can be — through the day-to-day actions of empowered individuals. This is what's worth fighting for in the school principalship.
>
> The challenge is to improve education in the only way it can be — through the day-to-day actions of empowered individuals.

Fullan's message is an unequivocal one: schools need to acquire the habit of self-development.

Building on Fullan's recent work, we want to make four central points:

1 The Developing School has to be more than just 'The Receiving School'

Some observers have claimed that the Developing School provides the **delivery system** for externally imposed changes such as those promulgated within the National Curriculum. Our argument is that this is not the complete picture. There will always be important changes generated outside schools to which they have to respond; and certainly the 'model' described in this book will enable schools to gain some control over, and purchase on, these 'externalized' changes. **Mandated ownership** is a phrase used in North America to describe the situation where a change is initiated outside the school, but then has to be 'adopted' (i.e. internalized and 'owned') by the receiving institution — a process which may well involve accommodations, modifications and 'local' agreements.

Does this, however, give the school enough power in the situation? Surely **pro-acting** is as important — if not more important — than **re-acting.** With Fullan's words still ringing in our ears (that schools make themselves healthy — by dint of their own efforts), we want to argue that:

- Schools must have the right and the responsibility for growing the internal capacity for change — the development culture. This is the **process** dimension.
- Schools must also have **some** discretion in terms of the agenda for change. While some of the focus areas will be 'given', the schools must have the opportunity not only to order priorities within three given areas, but also to include school-specific, staff-generated items on the change agenda. This is the content dimension.

Southworth (1987) has argued that the ability to exercise some power over both process and content enables a staff to experience **transformative collegiality** (as opposed to **normative collegiality** where the content agenda is predetermined).

2 The Developing School has to be developed

It is a question of keeping faith with the development philosophy. School development — as with each of its component parts within the supporting 'package deal' — has to be nurtured, grown and developed over time. As a consequence, the aim must be to exploit the school's natural resources — including its past achievements. It really is a case of integrating the best of the old with the best of the new. Above all, the development culture — the internal infrastructure for change — has to be grown and developed to provide the organic processing mechanism. As we have argued (and Fullan (1988) has underlined), the development culture provides the internal capacity for **positive vetting,** i.e. sifting and screening change initiatives. Schools should be searching for innovations:

'which ones are vital for us now?'
'which elements do we really need?'
'what are we doing already and will need only fine-tuning?'

3 In the Developing School, school development is not 'yet another initiative', it is *the* initiative

In other words, school development has to count; it has to mean a great deal to the staff members. It has to be seen as the core activity — built-in and not bolt-on or additive — through the agency of which all growth occurs. Staff commitment has to be visible and binding. Everyone has to believe in the **vision.** Moreover, the staff need to appreciate that having one central initiative (through which all others flow) actually reduces the pressures which arise from innovation overload. There will be fewer innovations; but there will be better innovation. Less is more, says Sizer (1984). The content/focus areas will be less demanding in sheer volume, but the process of development will be vastly superior. It is a question, at any one time, of developing a few areas really well.

4 In the Developing School, staff members are made responsible for developing their school

This can be both 'weighty' but liberating. The staff, generally, are the school developers. There is also a case, however, for having certain members of staff more directly responsible for the development work. Such roles could include:

a school/staff development coordinator;
membership of a school/staff development committee;
leader/chairperson/convenor of an interest group or working team;
curriculum coordinators, charged with the responsibility of supporting the implementation of the planned changes in particular curriculum areas.

Two of these roles are studied here in more detail.

a Staff Development Coordinator

A member of staff should be selected to fulfil the crucial role of Staff Development Coordinator. Such a person should:

(i) be a senior and/or experienced member of staff;
(ii) act as in-school coordinator and orchestrator of the development work;
(iii) have credibility in the eyes of the rest of the staff;
(iv) be able to form (and lead) a staff development committee as part of the internal infrastructure for the support and management of the development programmes;

(v) act as a link-person with the outside world/represent the school team at conferences, workshops and liaison meetings;
(vi) be prepared to act as both trainer and trainee (for example, with regard to the acquisition of evaluation skills/techniques);
(vii) provide linkage between the head and other staff members. If the head plays the coordinator role, then the issue of communication with staff will need to be considered.

b **Curriculum Coordinator**

Based on what has been said in earlier chapters, we can envisage a vital role concerning the orchestration of the implementation of the development work in a particular area of the school and/or curriculum. This is similar to the role of curriculum coordinator but involves acting as a 'teacher leader' as well. Key aspects of the 'teacher leader' role are suggested in the diagram below.

Figure 20:

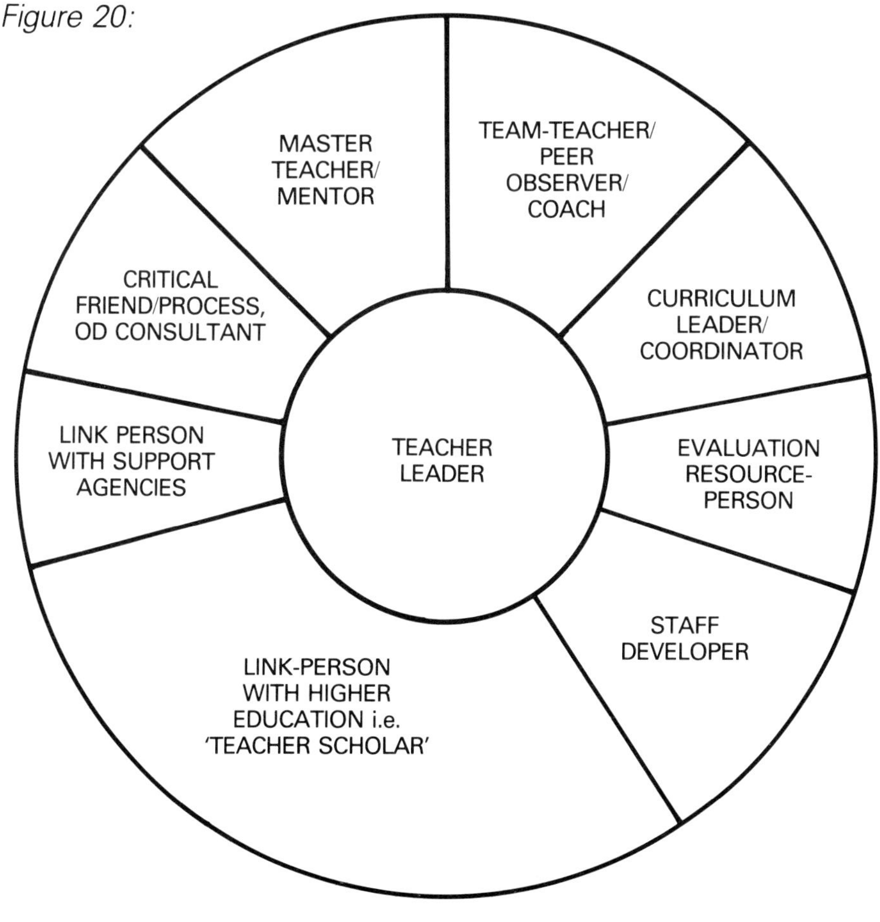

Developing School Development

Many commentators have argued that the process of innovation occurs over time and in different stages, which are often referred to as:

initiation
implementation
institutionalization

Moreover, school-based development is a complex package of innovations, all of which have to be 'developed'. Put simply, school-based development hinges around an internal process (as we have described above), which is used to effect the changes themselves. Consequently, in a particular school, both the internal process and the changes accruing may well be innovations. Although they are different kinds of innovations (the *process* and the *products* from the process), they have all to receive their due atention. They have all to be developed.

STAGES OF SCHOOL IMPROVEMENT
Typical Activities During Three Major Stages

Initiation	Implementation	Institutionalization
Deciding to start	Setting goals	Evaluating
Launching the process	Designing action plans	Building in the process
Needs assessment		Needed organizational changes
Developing commitment	Carrying out plans	

——————→

TIME

Some of the Factors Making for Success

Tie to a *local agenda* and high profile *local need*.

A clear, *well-structured model and process of change*.

An active *advocate* or champion (LEA and/or school) who understands the model and supports it.

Active *initiation* to start the innovation.

Good *quality* innovation.

Initiating School Development

Hopkins (1988) has used the table above to differentiate between initiation, implementation and institutionalization — as **stages of school improvement.** Looking at his list of typical activities, we are led to wonder whether there is, in fact, a fourth stage, called **preinitiation,** which involves preparing the ground for development. Maybe, also, 'deciding to start' and 'developing commitment' are activities to be undertaken at this preinitiation stage. Furthermore, we may choose to include 'setting goals' and 'designing action plans' as initiation (and not implementation) activities. It could also be argued that institutionalization begins *during* the earlier stages, i.e. during initiation and implementation. In other words, the process of innovation is complex and is certainly not as straightforward as any 'model' would suggest.

When Hopkins delineates some of the factors making for successful initiation, however, we feel that he is endorsing some of the central themes of this book.

Fullan (1986), in discussing the change process in schools, has made six vital points:

- avoid the rationality — or is it irrationality? — of 'brute sanity'; do not impose your bright ideas on those who do not consider them to be bright ideas;
- avoid innovation overload;
- be flexible in implementing the implementation plan (see chapter 2);
- attend to both content and process;
- use **pressure** and **support** to effect changes;
- remember that 'change' is a learning process (see chapter 1).

Concerning the initiation of school development, however, two further questions arise:

(a) What is the **level of initiation?**

Is the development work involving the whole staff or part of the staff (or, indeed, one or two individuals)? According to our thesis in this book, whole staff involvement needs to be galvanized from the outset if the Developing School is to become a reality. Even though the whole staff may not stay directly involved, they need to feel part of the development process. All their energies will need to be mobilized at some point. And they must all feel owners of the change agenda at the implementation stage.

(b) What are the most conducive trigger mechanisms for staff involvement?

Keep it close to reality (i.e. the classroom) is our advice. School development should never be allowed to stray too far from direct classroom concerns. After all, school development rests on classroom development.

What is clear, though, is that at the very beginning of the development work important decisions have to be taken concerning its initiation, management and planning (for implementation). How the school embarks on a development programme is crucial in itself. Holly and Martin (1987) have amended the following diagram to signal the nature of some of these decisions.

Figure 21: Profile of development

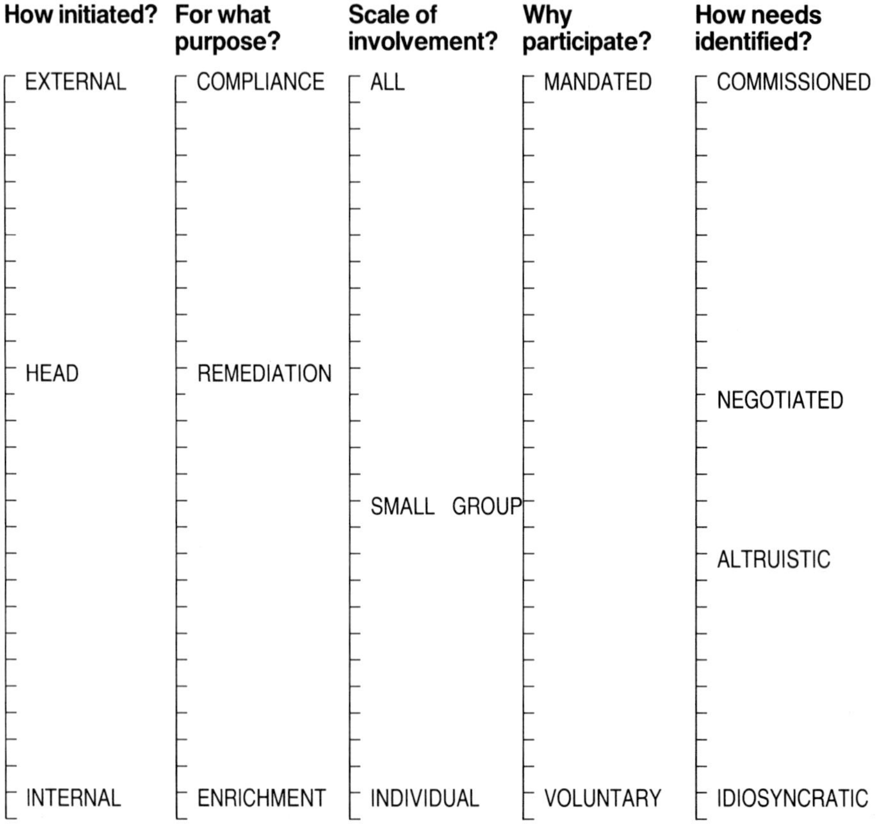

(Adapted from Fenstermacher and Berliner, 1985)

Over recent months one of us (see Holly, 1988) has been living with these questions in helping to launch an authority-wide programme for school development in Scotland. Referred to as the Programme of Evaluation in Grampian Schools (PEGS), it is a challenging attempt to encourage and support school-based development in over a dozen schools. Indeed, it is a rolling programme; more schools will enter next year and each year thereafter. The aims of the Programme are as follows:

AIMS OF THE PROGRAME

1. To enable schools to use self-evaluation for development purposes.
2. To provide opportunities for more collegial approaches to staff development.
3. To encourage the development of appropriate styles of school management.
4. To mobilize in schools the capacity for internal regeneration ie. school-driven improvement.
5. To integrate existing services and agencies within an external support partnership.
6. To stimulate professional reflection in order to enhance classroom processes.
7. To establish an appropriate management framework for enterprising schools.

The emphasis so far has been on **Getting Started.** While schools have been given a great deal of scope for their development work, the following suggestions have been made to them:

- Select different starting points.
- Remember the quality of the start is important.
- 'Start small, think big'; i.e. start with one or two areas of focus and build up later.
- Aim to develop a few areas really well.
- Keep it home-grown.
- Involve the staff early on; for example, in the identification of priority needs for development. In other words, start the sharing from the word 'go'.
- Think about the school's climate and its readiness for development, but do not let the answers prevent you starting. **Doing school development is the important thing.**
- Remember that the school is both a collection of classrooms and an organization. While both dimensions may well be in need of attention, one should not be over-accentuated to the detriment of the other.
- Resolve to acquire the 'long-haul mentality'. School development is akin to being 'a never ending story'. Consequently, the language used to describe the process is important. Terms like perserverance, orchestration, and coordination should be emphasized and reflected upon.
- Prepare the ground with the staff; enable them to 'buy in' to the

development work. Remember that 'involvement generates commitment' (see Goodchild and Holly, 1989).
- Marshall resources, especially time.
- Begin to think about both your support needs and your process training needs, for example, workshops in the use of evaluation techniques.
- Take seriously, and embark upon, the formulation of a School Development Plan.
- Prepare to be opportunistic in pursuit of this plan; it is often the case that development starts in 'lots of small ways'. Moreover, the application of different evaluative techniques may well lead into process considerations rather than vice versa.

More often than not, however, process considerations will be paramount; thus the emphasis on the planning process within school development (as described in chapter 2). What we would offer now, however, is a set of seven trigger questions to ask of the planning process:

- Is the plan owned jointly by the staff? Is there likely to be continuity of staffing? If not, what are the implications for the induction of new members of staff?
- Is the plan doable, i.e. implementable? Is it realistic and feasible? Is the plan focussed enough? Will it be a case of the staff

coping through scoping?

- Does the plan have enough built-in flexibility? Is the intention to keep faith with the staff's agenda that has been negotiated and agreed with them? Do the staff know where they stand and have they realistic expectations? Do they trust the plan?
- Are the staff ready to give up 'the two autonomies' (one being in favour of the child — the so-called 'progressive' influence — and the other in favour of the teacher — the 'traditional' orientation — see Richards, 1987) in favour of working together on the planning process in the best interests of the school as a collective? Is genuine staff collaboration a probability? a possibility? a far cry from present practice?
- Do the staff members appreciate that INSET needs flow out of priority needs for development and that *most* of the in-service activities that take place into the foreseeable future will have to be focussed on the developmental programme?
- Are the staff being encouraged to set targets for training tuned to the development work, but taking into consideration the

three levels of investment — individual, team and whole staff? Is there a balance between these levels which not only allows for the preservation of individual commitment, but also galvanizes whole school development? How much room is left for INSET related to career and personal needs? Is there an appropriate linkage here with staff appraisal?

- Is the 'management' of the school skilled enough both to empower others and to provide 'management for change' and change leadership? (see Goodchild and Holly, 1989). Are the staff members capable of breaking the bonds of 'value difference passivity' to explore constructively their value differences? Is the management/leadership style a conducive one?

Is this style:
participatory and consultative?;
capable of invoking staff commitment and co-ownership?;
encouraging and empowering?;
supportive and collaborative?;
facilitatory and enabling?;
orchestrative and integrative?;
team-oriented?;
capable of countenancing, and acting upon, criticism?;
exemplary?;
creative, enterprising and innovative?;
capable of providing change?;
indicative of 'learning' as opposed to 'teaching'?;

Does it matter if the 'dispersal model' applies and different schools with different capacities do different things with the same opportunity? Will 'good' schools get even better? Is this inequitable? What is more important equity or excellence/equality or quality? Should some schools be 'reined in' while other less dynamic schools are given additional help and resources?

Within these questions (and sub-questions) there are some central dilemmas; dilemmas which will have to be worked on and worked out by every staff in every participating school. To prescribe solutions would mean falling at the first fence and thus undermining the very essence of school-based development. It is noteworthy that someone who has spent some time researching into the process of School Development Planning should reach the following conclusions:

> I do not think that a school development plan in itself provides a blueprint for successful school development. Other factors are

> clearly at work, among which the ethos of the school, the personality, vitality and commitment of the head, and the willing and committed cooperation of the staff members are perhaps the most important. Given these, a plan may provide a flexible framework for school improvement, one that can take into account the specific needs of its pupils and the gifts of its teaching staff.
>
> Inevitably perhaps, I ended (the research) with more, and more complex, questions than those with which I began. Issues of school effectiveness, implementation, school culture, leadership and collegiality raised themselves. Among all these issues there is one that looms largest in my mind. The concept of a school development plan seems to imply an intrinsic collegiality which brings together headteacher, leadership and teachers' involvement as factors in school effectiveness. In encouraging collaborative working, moral questions about authority and responsibility are raised. The nature of authority needs to be understood by those holding it and accepting it, and the appropriate delegation of that authority must also be understood. Similarly the duties and responsibilities of collaborative working and collective decision making must be recognized and accepted in practice. A shift towards collegiality may disturb accepted group processes, upset the formal and informal relationships in a school.
>
> I wonder . . . how willing am I to face the possible tensions and conflicts that may arise if my professional colleagues and I choose to address these issues and examine our different approaches, methods, values and beliefs? (Campbell, 1987)

To round off this discussion of the initiation of school development work, it is appropriate to remind ourselves of the suggestions provided in the first three stages of the process outlined within GRIDS (Guidelines for Review and Internal Development in Schools):

STAGE 1 GETTING STARTED

1 Decide whether the GRIDS method is appropriate for your needs.
2 Consult the staff.
3 Decide how to manage the review and development.

STAGE 2 INITIAL REVIEW

1 Plan the initial review.
2 Prepare and distribute basic information.
3 Survey staff opinion.
4 Agree upon priorities for specific review and development.

STAGE 3 SPECIFIC REVIEW

1 Plan the specific review.
2 Find out what is the school's present policy/practice on the specific review topic.
3 Decide how effective present policy/practice actually is.
4 Agree conclusions and recommendations arising from the specific review.

Implementing School Development

Initiation leads to implementation; planning leads to doing. And implementation has to be sustained and continued over time until the new processes, products and practices become ingrained in the life of the school. Initiation can be exciting and invigorating. It represents the pursuit of the new. Implementation cannot make the same claims. It is when the going gets tough; when the new ideas have to be practised and made perfect. It demands the 'long-haul mentality'. It is when the irregular becomes much more regular. Sustenance and support, therefore, are crucial during implementation. It is a question of maintaining the enthusiasm and the drive when the excitement begins to wane: thus Fullan's emphasis of both continuing pressure and ongoing support.

Beyond Initiation

Initiation, then, is high-profile and stimulating. Implementation is something different. Initiation is about starting on the journey; implementation is the later part of the journey which is potentially more wearisome and mundane. Indeed, its very ordinariness works against it. Doing ordinary things (within implementation) lacks the allure of initiation. Given the current occurrence of innovation overload, in our darkest moments, we begin to think that Michael Fullan is right — 'implementation is a black-box'. It is a black box because we don't know much about it — partly because, in terms of the change process, we hardly ever get that far. Implementation represents uncharted waters. Most of our energies are spent on initiating new idea after new idea and just when we are ready to move into implementation of the first idea, the next idea comes along and demands attention. Each initiative takes the wind of the others; and each new initiative ensures that real implementation will remain illusory. All our time and energy is spent initiating . . . and initiating . . . and initiating. But initiation is the educational equivalent of 'fool's gold' — it flatters to deceive. It is not real change.

So what is real implementation? From the perspective of change theory, it is the stage during the overall process when plans are put into effect. It is the doing stage; the 'action for development' stage. According to Leavitt (1986), however, implementation is daily practice within an organization. It is what practitioners do; it is regular work. Real (as opposed to apparent) implementation, then, is a combination of these two interpretations; it is the stage in the change process when practitioners include the new ideas within their normal classroom practice. However, the word 'process' is often interpreted in different ways: it is the change process; what happens in classrooms and schools, i.e. the educational process; and the process of dissemination to, and acceptance by, the staff at large. During implementation, then, new ideas and practices are processed, thus impacting on educational processes and being adopted within a collegial process of staff affiliation. It is a question of 'getting all the players in the game'.

Above all, however, implementation is best characterized by the particular terminology used to describe it. It has various aspects: it is a question of:

forward movement; enacting the strategic plan; **doing development impact;**
- making it happen;
- making it stick;
- getting there;
- making a difference

continuing application; what are involved here are such facets as:
- perseverance
- persistence
- tenacity
- patience
- maintaining momentum
- unrelenting pressure
- commitment
- management

Management involves orchestration and the fusing of individual and small-team enterprise with *the* enterprise — the whole school.

It is a question of attaining the level of **critical mass** in support of change

- **changing practice;** doing new things and thus 'going against the grain';
- **support;** positive reinforcement, empowerment, coaching, training and applied INSET.

More than anything else, however, implementation is the cornerstone of the change process; it is when changes actually occur. It involves ringing the changes in educational practice. It is worth noting that the process framework offered in this book is none other than a reformulation of the change process itself. As a consequence, the process guidelines arising from GRIDS emphasize the action orientation of implementation:

STAGE 4 ACTION FOR DEVELOPMENT

1. Plan the development work.
2. Consider how best to meet the in-service needs of the teachers involved in the development.
3. Move into action.
4. Assess the effectiveness of the development work.

STAGE 5 OVERVIEW AND RE-START

1. Plan the overview.
2. Decide whether the changes introduced at the development stage should be made permanent.
3. Decide whether this approach to school review and development should be continued or adapted.
4. Restart the cycle.
5. Decide if you want to inform anyone else about what happened in the first cycle.

Hopkins (1988), in describing the 'experience of change', has underlined many of the points raised above:

> Change at the individual level is a process whereby individuals alter their ways of thinking and doing. It is a process of developing new skills and above all finding meaning and satisfaction in new ways of doing things. This implies:
>
> (1) that change takes place over time;
> (2) that the initial stages of any significant change always involve anxiety and uncertainty;
> (3) that ongoing technical and psychlogical support assistance is crucial if the anxiety is to be coped with;
> (4) that change involves learning new skills through practice and feedback — it is incremental and developmental:
> (5) that the most fundamental breakthrough occurs when

people can cognitively understand the underlying conception and rationale with respect to 'why this new way works better';

(6) that organizational conditions within the school (peer norms, administrative leadership) and in relation to the school (for example, external administrative support and technical help) make it more or less likely that the process will succeed;

(7) successful change involves pressure, but it is pressure through interaction with peers and other technical and administrative leaders.

Building on the work of Michael Fullan, Hopkins (1988) has also listed the 'factors related to effective/ineffective implementation':

Factors Related to Implementation

CHARACTERISTICS OF THE INNOVATION

1 Need for the change
2 Clarity, complexity and scope of the change
3 Quality and availability of materials
4 Nature of initiation decision

CHARACTERISTICS AT THE SCHOOL SYSTEM LEVEL

5 History of innovative attempts
6 Expectations and training for heads
7 Teacher professional development
8 External support
9 Planning; including a realistic time line and monitoring
10 Overload

CHARACTERISTICS AT THE SCHOOL LEVEL

11 Heads' actions
12 Teacher/teacher relations and actions
13 Parental and community involvement

FACTORS EXTERNAL TO THE SCHOOL SYSTEM

14 Teacher Industrial Action
15 Demographic Factors
16 Changes in Funding

IMPLEMENTATION STRATEGIES

17 Inservice Training linked to the problems of implementation
18 Monitoring and Feedback
19 Attention to components of Implementation
20 School Development Plan.

In the Developing School, implementation is crucial. It makes develoment happen; it is the central process for producing the intended outcomes. Indeed, this process-product orientation is its greatest contribution to school development. For the kind of impact demanded by the Developing School, however, *all* the staff have to be involved at the implementation stage. They are all implementers; they are all practising the ideas, taking action on the strength of them and incorporating them into normal, everyday classroom processes. During implementation, then, the scale of engagement becomes a central concern. During initiation, it is possible to 'box cleverly' and involve staff members in different permutations — in planning teams, interest groups, etc. During the planning/initiation phase, therefore, while all the staff should be involved periodically, the whole staff should not be involved all the time. Implementation, though, is down to everyone. It may well be a question, therefore, of galvanizing new enthusiasms, new commitments and new excitements. Maybe this is especially the case in the early days of implementation. Perhaps, it is also a case of differentiating between early implementation and later implementation. The latter undoubtedly fades into institutionalization, at which point **routine use** is the key factor.

Institutionalization, from one perspective, is tantamount to the embeddedness of the new ideas within classroom practice across the staff at large. This is, however, only one side of the equation. It is not just a case of the installation of new practices, however; it is vital to institutionalize the process framework which is part and parcel of the development culture. The development culture, then, provides the framework for institutionalizing the products of the change process; but the process itself — plus the development culture — also has to be incorporated within the mainstream life of the school.

Prolonged implementation then, involves continuation and, thus, **institutionalization.** And, as Hopkins maintains in the chart included earlier in this chapter, at the institutionalization stage, it is vital to evaluate the progress of the process of development. It is time to evaluate the quality of the various outcomes — the products of school development.

It is interesting to note that Leithwood, Fullan and Heald-Taylor (1987) have advised that attempts should be made to simplify the process of educational change by breaking the process into phases — more manageable chunks. The same authors recommend that planned educational change be organized around five main phases:

(i) preparing for school improvement/development;

i(ii) determining specific goals;
(iii) selecting or developing the solutions;
(iv) implementing the solutions;
(v) institutionalizing the solutions.

While they add that evaluation and planning continue throughout the process, they stress that, at the institutionalization stage, **summative monitoring** is called for.

As mentioned above, Holly and Hopkins (1988) have differentiated between evaluation as, evaluation for and evaluation of. 'Evaluation as' can be associated with the planning and reviewing process; 'evaluation for' with formative feedback during implementation; and 'evaluation of' with assessment of the long-term success of the implementation of the new ideas.

As mentioned in an earlier chapter, the evaluation of school development could be based on performance indicators generated from within the development process.

> **Learning outcomes constitute the acid test for school development.**

And this brings us full circle. We began this book by arguing for the centrality of learning within the Learning School. The Developing School has, at heart, a fixation with the **Learning Level.** Hutchins (1988), building on the work of Bela Banathy, has argued, from a 'systems' perspective, that there are five such domains: the societal level, the institutional level, the administrative/managerial level, the instructional (teaching) level and the learning level, but that the latter is the primary level and the one around which the others should revolve. As a consequence, he says, teachers should be encouraged to do **backward mapping** from the learning level; i.e. they should work out which teaching styles and approaches can best be deployed to enhance and support the learning level. Moreover, they should look at their schools as organizations in the same light. The question to ask of both teaching and organizational arrangements is **do they enhance children's learning?**

The object, then, is to design schooling according to criteria suggested by children's learning. Each school should aim to become a learning community. Co-learning, involving staff members, the children and their parents and friends from the local community, is the goal. Participation, involvement and cooperation are the watch-words. Life-long learning is the key.

Moreover, as we emphasized in chapter 1, the school as an organization has to celebrate learning by providing appropriate structures for its pursuit. The Developing School learns how to encourage learning.

In relation to the Developing School, the Learning School is both the process and the product.

References

ALEXANDER, R. (1984) *Primary School Teaching,* London, Holt, Rinehart and Winston.
ARGYRIS, C. and SCHON, D. (1978) *Organizational Learning: A Theory of Action Perspective,* Reading, MA, Addison-Wesley.
BALL, S. (1987) *The Micro-politics of the School,* London, Methuen.
BENNIS, W. and NANUS, B. (1985) *Leaders: Strategies for Taking Charge,* New York, Harper and Row.
BENYON, L. (1982) 'Curriculum continuity', *Education 3-13,* 9, 2, pp.36-41.
BERMAN, P. and MCLAUGHLIN, M. (1976) 'Implementation of educational innovation', *Forum,* 40, pp.345-70.
BIOTT, C. (1988) 'Collaborative enquiry in staffrooms and seminars', *Forum,* 30, 2, spring, pp.56-8.
BLOCK, J.A. *et al* (1983) 'Institutionalized in-service training for science teachers', *European Journal of Science Education,* 5, 2, pp.157-69.
BLOCK, P. (1987) *The Empowered Manager,* San Francisco, Jossey-Bass.
BRENNAN, E.J.T. (1985) 'On the eve of CPVE: Some impressions of the changing pre-vocational scene', *Cambridge Journal of Education,* 15, 1.
CAMPBELL, P. (1987) *School Development Plans,* report prepared for the Suffolk Education Authority and the Cambridge Institute of Education, mimeo.
CAMPBELL, R.J. (1985) *Developing the Primary School Curriculum,* London, Holt, Rinehart and Winston.
CARNEGIE REPORT (1986).
CHARTERS, W.W. and JONES, J.E. (1973) 'On the risk of appraising non-events in program evaluation, *Educational Researcher,* November.
CLERKIN, C. (1985) 'What do primary school heads actually do all day?', *School Organization,* 5, 4, pp.287-300.
COULSON, A.A. (1976) 'The Role of the primary head' in PETERS, R.S. (Ed) *The Role of the Head,* London, Routledge and Kegan Paul.
COULSON, A.A. (1986) *The Managerial Work of Primary School Headteachers,* Sheffield Papers in Education Manager, No. 48, Sheffield City Polytechnic.
COURT, G. (1987) *Of Primary Importance,* Tower Hamlets Primary Teacher Support Project.
CRAIG, I. (1987) 'Using time efficiently' In CRAIG, I. (Ed). *Primary School Management in Action,* London, Longman, chapter 5.

CUBAN, L. (1987) *How Teachers Taught Constancy and Change in American Classrooms,* New York, Longman.
DALIN, P. (1988) Speech on 'School-based development', *Grampian Educational Authority,* September.
DALIN, P. and RUST, V. (1983) *Can Schools Learn?* Windsor, NFER-Nelson.
DAY, C., JOHNSTON, D. and WHITAKER, P. (1985) *Managing Primary Schools,* London, Harper and Row.
DEAL, T. and KENNEDY, A. (1983) 'Culture and school performance, *Educational Leadership,* 40, 5, pp.14-15.
DEAN, J. (1980) 'Continuity' in RICHARDS, C. (Ed). *Primary Education: Issues for the Eighties,* London, A & C Black, pp.42-52.
DEPARTMENT OF EDUCATION AND SCIENCE (1977) *Ten Good Schools: A Secondary School Enquiry by HMI,* London, HMSO.
DEPARTMENT OF EDUCATION AND SCIENCE (1978a) *Making INSET Work: In-service Education and Training for Teachers. A Basis for Discussion,* London, HMSO.
DEPARTMENT OF EDUCATION AND SCIENCE (1978b) *Primary Education in England: A Survey by HM Inspectors of Schools,* London, HMSO.
DEPARTMENT OF EDUCATION AND SCIENCE (1982) *Mathematics Counts* (The Cockroft Report), London, HMSO.
DEPARTMENT OF EDUCATION AND SCIENCE (1987) *Primary Schools: Some Aspects of Good Practice,* (An HMI Publication), London, HMSO.
EASON, P. (1985) *Making School-centred INSET Work,* London, Croom Helm with The Open University Press.
EISNER, E. (1985) *The Art of Educational Evaluation,* Lewes, Falmer Press.
ELLIOT, J., BRIDGES, D., EBBUTT, D., GIBSON, R. and NIAS, J. (1981) *School Accountability,* London, Grant McIntyre.
FENSTERMACHER, G.D. and BERLINER, D.C. (1985) 'Determining the value of staff development', *The Elementary School Journal,* 85, 3, pp.281-314.
FINLAYSON, D.C. (1973) 'Measuring school climate', *Trends in Education,* April, pp.19-27.
FRASER, B. and FISHER, D. (1983) 'Use of actual and referred CES in person-environment fit research', *Journal of Educational Psychology,* 75, pp.303-11.
FULLAN, M. (1985) 'Change processes and strategies at the local level', *Elementary School Journal,* 85, 3, pp.394-421.
FULLAN, M. (1986) 'Improving of the implementation of educational school organization', *Elementary School Journal,* 6, 3, pp.321-6.
FULLAN, M. (1987) *Managing Curriculum Change in Curriculum at the Crossroads,* London, SCDC.
FULLAN, M. (1988) *What's Worth Fighting for in the Principalship?,* Toronto, Ontario Public School Teachers' Federation.
GOODACRE, E. (1984) 'Postholders and language assertiveness', *Education 3-13,* 12, 1, pp.17-21.
GOODCHILD, S.R. and HOLLY, P. (1989) *Management for Change: The Garth Hill Experience,* Lewes, Falmer Press.
GOODLAD, J.I. (1972) 'Staff development: The league model', *Theory into Practice,* xi, 4, pp.207-14.
GOODLAD, J.I. (Ed) (1987) *The Ecology of School Renewal,* Chicago, IL, University of Chicago Press.

GOODLAD, J.I. and KLEIN, M.F. (1970) *Looking Behind the Classroom Door,* Worthington, OH, Charles E. Jones.

GUSKEY, T.R. (1986) 'Staff development and the process of teacher change', *Educational Researcher,* 15, 5.

HALPIN, A. and CROFT, D. (1982) 'The organization climate of schools', (USOE Research Project), August.

HALL, G.E. and LOUCKS, S. (1977) 'A developmental model for determining whether the treatment is actually implemented', *American Educational Research Journal,* 14, 3, pp.263-76.

HANDY, C. (1987) 'By way of encouragement: The path to a better society', *Royal Society of the Arts Journal,* CXXXVI, 5377.

HARGREAVES, D. (1982) *The Challenge for the Comprehensive School,* London, Routledge and Kegan Paul.

HARGREAVES, D. (1988) 'Education Change and In-service Training', Speech to British Council Course, Girton College, September.

HOLLY, P.J. (1983) 'On the outskirts: Educational action-research', unpublished MA thesis, Cambridge Institute of Education.

HOLLY, P.J. (1984) 'The institutionalization of action-research in schools', *Cambridge Journal of Education,* 14, 2, pp.5-18.

HOLLY, P.J. (1985) 'The developing school', *TRIST/CIE Working Paper.*

HOLLY, P.J. (1986a) 'Soaring like turkeys — The impossible dream? Managing change for school improvement, *School Organisation,* 6, 3.

HOLLY, P.J. (1986b) 'Teachers learning about learning INSET materials for staff discussion', *CIE/TRIST.*

HOLLY, P.J. (1986c) 'The teachers GUIDE', *CIE/TRIST Working Paper.*

HOLLY, P.J. (1987) 'Teaching for learning: Learning for teaching?', *Curriculum,* 8, 2, pp.15-23.

HOLLY, P.J. (1989) 'Programme of evaluation in Grampian Schools: Introductory paper'.

HOLLY, P.J. and MARTIN, D. (1987) 'A head start? Primary schools and the TRIST experience', *Cambridge Journal of Education,* 17, 3, pp.186-96.

HOLLY, P.J. and WIDEEN, M. (1987) 'Cultural perspective on institutionalization', Paris, OECD/CDRI.

HOLLY, P.J. and HOPKINS, D. (1988) 'Evaluation and school improvement', *Cambridge Journal of Education,* 18, 2, pp.221-45.

HOLLY, P.J. and NEWMAN, K. (1988) 'Evaluation within the SGTE initiative in Northamptonshire: Introductory paper', Cambridge Institute of Education, Northamptonshire LEA.

HOLLY, P.J., JAMES, T. and YOUNG, J. (1987) *DELTA Project: The Experience of TRIST,* London, Manpower Services Commission.

HOPKINS, D. (Ed) (1986) *Inservice Training and Educational Development,* London, Croom Helm.

HOPKINS, D. (1988) Speech on the change process, Cambridge Institute of Education.

HOUSE OF COMMONS SELECT COMMITTEE (1986) *Achievement in Primary Schools,* Vol.1, London, HMSO.

HOYLE, E. (1975) 'The creativity of the school in Britain' in HARRIS, A. *et al* (Eds.) *Curriculum Innovation,* London, Croom Helm/Open University Press.

HOYLE, E. (1986) *The Politics of School Management,* London, Hodder and Stoughton.

HUGHES, M. (1985) 'Leadership in professionally staffed organizations' in HUGHES, M., RIBBINS, P. and THOMAS, H., *Managing Education: The System and the Institution,* London, Holt, Rinehart and Winston.

HUTCHINS, C.L., (1988) 'Design as the Missing Piece in Education', conference paper, School-Year, 2020, Aspen, October.

ILEA (1985) *Improving Primary Schools* (Report of the Committee on Primary Education) (The 'Thomas Report'), London, ILEA.

ILEA (1986) *The Junior School Project: A Summary of the Main Report,* London, ILEA Research and Statistics Branch.

JOYCE, B. *et al* (1983) *The Structure of School Improvement,* New York, Longman.

JOYCE, B. and SHOWERS, B. (1980) 'Improving in-service training: The messages of research, *Educational Leadership,* 37, 5, pp.379-86.

JOYCE, B. and SHOWERS, B. (1982) 'The coaching of teaching', *Educational Leadership,* 40, 1, pp.4-10.

JOYCE, B. and MCKIBBIN, M. (1982) 'Teacher growth states and school environments', *Educational Leadership,* 40, 2, pp.36-41.

LEAVITT, H.J. (1986) *Corporate Pathfinders,* Homewood, IL, Dow Jones-Irwin.

LEITHWOOD, K., FULLAN, M. and HEALD-TAYLOR, G. (1987) 'School level CRDI procedures to guide the school improvement process', mimeo.

LIEBERMAN, A. (1986) 'Collaborative research: Working with, not working on', *Educational Leadership,* February, pp.28-32.

LIEBERMAN, A. (1988) 'Expanding the leadership team', *Educational Leadership,* 45, 5, pp.4-8.

LIEBERMAN, A. and MILLER, L. (1981) 'Highlights of research on improving schools', *Educational Leadership.*

LITTLE, J.W. (1981) 'School success and staff development: The role of staff development in urban desegregated schools', final report to National Institute of Education.

MCLAUGHLIN, M. and MARSH, D. (1987) Summary of the findings of the Rand Corporation.

MCMAHON, A. *et al* (1984) *GRIDS Handbooks,* York, Longman/Schools Council.

MCNEIL, L. (1988) 'Contradictions of control, Part 1: Administrators and teachers', *Phi Delta Kappa,* January, pp.333-9.

MANASSE, A.L. (1985) 'Improving conditions for principal effectiveness: Policy implications of research', *Elementary School Journal,* 85, 3.

MILLER, L. (1988) 'A tale of two schools', speech from Puget Sound Educational Consortium, Seattle, August.

MOOS, R.H. (1974) *The Social Climate Scales: An overview,* Palo Alto, CA, Consulting Psychologists' Press.

MORTIMORE, P., SAMMONS, P., STOLL, L., LEWIS, D. and ECOB, R. (1988) *School Matters,* Frome, Open Books.

NAISBITT, J. (1984) *Megatrends,* London, Futura.

NATIONAL UNION OF TEACHERS (1979) *Middle Schools: Deemed or Doomed?* London, NUT.

NIAS, D.J. (1987) 'One finger, one thumb: A case study of the deputy head's part in the leadership of a nursery/infant school' in SOUTHWORTH, G.W. (Ed). *Readings in Primary School Management,* Lewes, Falmer Press, pp.30-53.

NIAS, D.J., SOUTHWORTH, G.W. and YEOMANS, R. (1989) *Primary School Staff Relationships: A Study of School Culture,* London, Cassell.

NISBET, J. (1974) 'Strengthening the creativity of the school'. *Creativity of the School,* a CERI Publication, Paris, OECD.

OPEN UNIVERSITY (1988) 'Management roles and responsibilities' in *Managing Schools: Leadership and Decision making in School,* Block 2, Part 2, Course E325, Milton Keynes, Open University Press, pp.31-70.

PATTERSON, J.L., PURKEY, S.C. and PARKER, J.V. (1986) *Productive School Systems for a Non-rational World,* Alexandria, VA, Association for Supervision and Curriculum Development (ASCD).

PETERS, T. (1987) *Thriving in Chaos,* London, Macmillan.

PETERS, T.J. and WATERMAN, R.H. (1982) *In Search of Excellence,* New York, Harper and Row.

PETERS, T., and AUSTIN, N. (1985) *A Passion for Excellence: The Leadership Difference,* London, Fontana.

POLLARD, A., and TANN, S. (1988) *Reflective Teaching in the Primary School: A Handbook for the Classroom,* London, Cassell.

PRIMARY SCHOOL RESEARCH AND DEVELOPMENT GROUP/SCHOOLS COUNCIL (1984) *Curriculum Responsibility and the Use of Teacher Expertise in the Primary School,* Birmingham, University of Birmingham, Dept. of Curriculum Studies.

REID, K., HOPKINS, D. and HOLLY, P.J. (1987) *Towards the Effective School,* Oxford, Basil Blackwell.

RICHARDS, C. (1986) 'The curriculum from 5 to 16: Background, content and some implications for primary education', *Education 3-13,* 14, 1, pp.3-8.

RICHARDS, C. (1987) 'Primary education in England: An analysis of some recent issues and developments', *Curriculum,* 8, 1.

ROPER, S., DEAL, T. and DORNBUSCH, S. (1976) 'Collegial evaluation of classroom teaching: Does it work?, *Educational Research Quarterly,* spring, pp. 56-66.

RUBIN, L. (1978) *The In-Service Education of Teachers, Trends, Processes, and Prescriptions,* Boston, MA, Allyn and Bacon.

SAGOR, R. (1981) 'A day in the life — A Technique for Assessing School Climate and Effectiveness', *Educational Leadership,* December, pp.190-3.

SARASON, S.B. (1971) *The Culture of the School and the Problem of Change,* Boston, MA, Allyn and Bacon.

SAXL, E., LIEBERMAN, A. and MILES, M.B. (1987) 'Help is at hand: New knowledge for teachers as staff developers', *Journal of Staff Development,* 8, 1, pp.7-11.

SCHAEFER, R. (1967) *The School as a Centre of Inquiry,* New York, Harper and Row.

SCHON, D.A. (1971) *Beyond the Stable State,* London, Temple Smith.

SCHON, D.A. (1983) *The Reflective Practitioner,* London, Temple Smith.

SCHON, D.A. (1987) *Educating the Reflective Practitioner,* San Francisco, CA, Jossey-Bass.

SKILBECK, M. (1976) 'School-based curriculum development and teacher education' in PRESCOTT, W. and BOLAM, R. *Supporting Curriculum Development,* Milton Keynes, Open University Press.

SIZER, T.R. (1984) *Horace's Compromise. The Dilemma of the American High School,* Boston, MA, Houghton Mifflin.

SMITH, L.M. *et al* (1986) *Educational Innovators: Then and Now,* Lewes, Falmer Press.

SOUTHWORTH, G.W. (1984) 'Development of staff in primary schools: Some ideas and implications', *British Journal of In-Service Education,* 10, 3, pp.6-15.

SOUTHWORTH, G.W. (1985a) 'The headteacher as a supply teacher', *Education,* 1 March, p.181.

SOUTHWORTH, G.W. (1985b) 'Changing Management in Primary Schools', *Education,* 22 November, p.470.

SOUTHWORTH, G.W. (1986) 'The primary head's burden', *Education,* 1 August, p.109.

SOUTHWORTH, G.W. (1987a) 'Primary school headteachers and collegiality' in SOUTHWORTH, G.W., (Ed) *Readings in Primary School Management,* Lewes, Falmer Press.

SOUTHWORTH, G.W. (1987b) *Readings in Primary School Management,* Lewes, Falmer Press.

SOUTHWORTH, G.W. (1988) 'Looking at leadership: English primary school Headteachers at Work', *Education 3-13.*

SOUTHWORTH, G.W. and MYER, J. (1988) 'Follow my leader', *Education,* 4 March, p.186.

SPARKS, G.M. (1983) 'Synthesis of research on staff development for effective teaching', *Educational Leadership,* 41, 3, pp.65-72.

STEERS, (1977) *Organisational Effectiveness,* Santa Monica, Goodyear.

STENHOUSE, L. (1975) *An Introduction to Curriculum Research and Development,* London, Heinemann.

SYKES, G. (1988) Speech to Paget Sound Educational Consortium, Seattle, August.

TAYLOR, P.H. (1986) *Expertise and the Primary Teacher,* Windsor, NFER/Nelson.

THOMAS, N. (1987) 'Team spirit', *Child Education,* January, pp.10-11.

TIKUNOFF, W., WARD, B. and GRIFFIN, G. (1979) *Interactive Research and Development on Teaching: Final Reports,* San Francisco, CA, Far West Laboratory.

TIMAR, T.B. and KIRP, D.L. (1987) 'Educational reform and institutional competence', *Harvard Educational Review,* 57, 3, pp.308-30.

TORBERT, W.R. (1976) *Creating a Community of Inquiry: Conflict, Collaboration, Transformation,* New York, John Wiley.

TORRINGTON, D., WEIGHTMAN, J. and JOHNS, K. (1987) 'Doing well but could do better', *Times Educational Supplement,* 30 October.

TOYNBEE, H. (1987) 'The management of collaborative teaching', in CRAIG, I. (Ed) *Managing the Primary Classroom,* London, Longman.

WADE, R.K. (1985) 'What makes a difference in in-service teacher education? A meta-analysis of research', *Educational Leadership,* p.48-54.

WATERS, D. (1987) 'The deputy as trainee head' in CRAIG I. (Ed) *Primary School Management in Action,* London, Longman.

WEICK, K.E. (1976) 'Education organizations as loosely-coupled systems', *Administrative Science Quarterly,* 21, pp.1-19.

WHITAKER, P. (1983) *The Primary Head,* London, Heinemann.
WOOD, F.H. and THOMPSON, S.R. (1980) 'Guidelines for better staff development', *Educational Leadership,* 37, 5, pp.374-8.

Index